GROWING WITH THE C.

The author and some of the characters from 'Growing with the Grain':

Top left: Wilf; Top centre: the author, 'Davy', or 'Nipper';
Top right: Fred; Bottom left: Luke;
Bottom centre: Mr Chubb, farm manager; Bottom right: Cecil

Growing with the Grain

Richard Mack

Illustrations by Jill Mack

EX LIBRIS PRESS

Published in 1997 by
EX LIBRIS PRESS
1 The Shambles
Bradford on Avon
Wiltshire

Design and typesetting by
Ex Libris Press

Typeset in 10 point Times

Cover printed by
Shires Press
Trowbridge
Wiltshire

Printed in Britain by
Cromwell Press
Broughton Gifford
Wiltshire

ISBN 0 978548 88 2

To Jill

CONTENTS

'... *Mumbling my explanations, delicately tiptoeing barefoot over the expensive carpet, hoping the remains of the effluent clung to my trousers, I retired to the sanctuary of the bathroom ...*' – see page 77.

1.

From Rhubarb to Capons

G ARDENER WANTED, MUST BE YOUNG AND FIT, the advertisement in the local paper ran, 'and,' it continued mysteriously, 'be prepared to undertake other duties.' It sounded a likely prospect. I rang the number given and, without further inquiry, secured an interview for the following day.

The job was at a guest house on the outskirts of a small town eight miles from my home. I borrowed my mother's old Morris Minor and set off for my interview, slightly apprehensive, wondering what to expect. I had never had a job before, let alone an interview.

The Hoad Hill Guest House was a large, seedy-looking building set in the middle of a row of houses on the main road leading into town. A narrow pavement ran alongside it; there was little hint of the garden, which was, I assumed, at the rear and probably, in the manner of town gardens, tiny.

My ring on the tarnished brass bell was answered by an elderly maid, resplendent in an old-fashioned uniform redolent of an age long passed. I explained my business and she let me into a gloomy hall, showing me to a brown, leather-covered armchair.

'I'll fetch Miss Florence directly.' she said and vanished down a long, dark, dusty passageway.

I looked around the hall. There were several more brown leather armchairs and a sofa, similarly clad. The leather was dry and cracked and, in places, crudely patched. An oak table, laden with old magazines, stood in the centre and high above it hung an ornate chandelier, covered with dust and cobwebs. It seemed an austere room and I wondered where all the guests had gone, for the place was as quiet and still as a tomb.

I was shaken out of my reverie by a solid clumping of feet and from the same passageway down which the maid had disappeared emerged a small, energetic woman in her early seventies. She was a little over five feet tall, broad in the shoulders and hips and generously endowed both in front and behind. She was dressed in a tweed skirt, a thick Army-style shirt covered by a brown cardigan, her hands thrust deep into the pockets. Her sensible, leather-soled, slightly muddy brogues were scuffed and down at heel and a brown beret adorned her head. Her short bowed legs were clad in thick stockings that looked as though they had been inexpertly hand-knitted.

She smiled at me, and I rose to my feet, guessing correctly she was Miss Jeffries, co-owner of the Hoad Hill Guest House. We shook hands and she took me to her office which overlooked the garden. This was no town garden. The closely built houses lining the road were a sham: there was a vast area of ground behind, sloping gently down to a river and, at a rough estimate, the garden of the guest house encompassed about two acres.

When I had left my public school in the autumn of 1961, I had no clear idea of what I wanted to do with the rest of my life, other than an ill-defined leaning towards agriculture. I was living with my parents who were becoming increasingly agitated that their expensively educated son showed little interest in pursuing a career or even starting to earn a wage. The gardening job, I thought, might earn me some respite, some money and a measure of independence. My only worry was that Miss Jeffries would realise I hardly intended to make my career working in the garden of her guest house.

She pulled up a chair for me in front of an untidy desk and lowered her enormous bottom onto a creaking swivel chair on the other side. I felt like an errant schoolboy in the headmaster's study about to endure a reprimand which would surely end with the familiar words 'this will hurt me more than it will hurt you', and I had to remind myself the dreary days of my

8

academic education were finished: this was the adult world where my real education would start.

Miss Jeffries shuffled some papers around the desk and uncovered a silver cigarette box. Carefully selecting a cigarette, she courteously offered me the box, but I declined. Quite apart from the fact I did not smoke and an innate feeling it would be wrong to do so at such a time, I dimly remembered the advice of one of the masters at my recently left school: never smoke at an interview. It was, I reflected, the only advice I had received on how to conduct myself at such an important event.

Miss Jeffries leant back in her swivel chair, drawing on her cigarette with the satisfaction of the true addict and outlined the job for me. The hotel, she said, was for elderly guests who regarded it as their home. She ran the place with her twin sister, Doris. The two acres of garden helped supplement the menu, giving a measure of self-sufficiency. In addition to vegetables there was a small herd of goats, hens and, penned at the bottom of the garden, half-a-dozen pigs which lived off the waste food. Doris ran the garden, which seemed to me more of a smallholding than a garden, and Florence the hotel. I was beginning to understand the meaning of 'other duties'.

'Now,' said Florence, 'we come to you. With your qualifications and background I do not see you staying at the Hoad Hill Guest House as the resident gardener for the rest of your days.'

It was the moment I had feared, the flaw in my application.

'We have both been guilty of a small deception,' she continued. 'You are endeavouring to convince me you want a permanent job when I know perfectly well you do not and, conversely, I have no permanent position to offer.' She waved her hand in the air, scattering cigarette ash dangerously over her paperwork. 'It's the digging I want done. Albert, my full-time gardener, is too old: another winter of digging would kill the poor man and, God knows, we have enough deaths in this place without adding Albert to the list.'

She stubbed her cigarette out in the ashtray and leant forward across the crowded desk.

'I didn't advertise the job as temporary' she told me 'for I did not think anyone would be interested, so I will make a bargain with you. The job is yours provided you can promise me you will finish the digging before you leave to make some use of your qualifications. What do you say?'

I agreed immediately and she stood up and shook my hand.

'Well done,' she said. 'You start tomorrow. I'll take you down the garden to meet Doris.'

As we left her office she said over her shoulder, rather unflatteringly I thought, 'You were the only applicant anyway.'

ଔ

Doris was Florence's identical twin sister, identical in every respect except for her clothing. She sported a brown beret on her head, the same as her sister, but there the similarity ended. Whatever clothing she wore was covered by a brown mackintosh, devoid of buttons and fastened around the middle by a piece of binder twine. A pair of black Wellington boots reached to the hem of her macintosh: I wondered if they had been specially made to cope with her bowed legs. We shook hands. The strength of her grip and the prickly hardness of her dirt-ingrained skin against my tender soft hand, more used to holding a pen than a spade, surprised me. I felt as though I had been rasped by a coarse file as she withdrew her hand.

Florence left me with Doris, solidly clumping her way back to the house. Doris eyed me as she inserted a cigarette into a long holder.

'You are very young,' she said after she had lit her cigarette.

'What do your parents think of you becoming a gardener?'

I really had no idea, though I suspected the short answer was 'not very much'.

'I am sure they will be delighted when I tell them you have given me the job,' I replied diplomatically. Doris smiled. 'Come, I will show you around.'

She showed me her goats, half a dozen nannies, evidently her pride and joy. She showed me the eight pigs housed in concrete pens at the very bottom of the garden and she showed me the rhubarb bed, covered by a tangle of weeds which, to my untoured eye, extended to about half an acre. Finally, she showed me the hens, scratching around in a large wire netted run. The hens were enormous. 'Capons,' Doris remarked. 'Our guests love them. We keep a seperate flock, over there, for eggs.'

I wondered if this peculiar mixture of eggs, capons, pork, goats' milk and rhubarb was an eccentric recipe for prolonging life or whether it hastened the departure of the guests. It seemed unwise to ask Doris so early in my gardening career, but I did ask her how her guests managed to consume such a vast amount of rhubarb – from the size of the bed they must have had to eat it for breakfast, lunch and tea.

Doris laughed. 'We're famous for our rhubarb,' she said, ejecting her cigarette stub from her holder with a clever twist of her wrist. 'In the season we sell it to greengrocers around the area and we bottle our surplus so we have a year round supply.' She smiled. 'It has a certain beneficial laxative effect on our guests.'

She introduced me to Albert, who was sweeping leaves into ragged burning piles. He was a thin old man with a mean looking face. Albert grunted without looking up, concentrating on his work with unnecessary application. The piles of leaves reminded me of miniature smoking volcanoes, the occasional flickers of flame adding to the illusion, the sun's rays shining weakly through the choking smoke, illuminating Albert's unconscious version of a scene from hell.

'You mustn't worry about Albert, ' Doris told me. 'He has been with us since we started the guest house over thirty years ago. He cannot accept he is an old man now. He planted the rhubarb crowns when we came here and he has tended them,weeded them and dug the ground until he had his operation last year. Now he watches the weeds taking over, suffocating his beloved bed, helpless to carry out a task he performed so easily when he was fitter. Perfection is so temporary,' she continued, 'and it grieves him to see nature contemptuously erasing thirty years of work in such a short time. Albert is an obstinate man, preferring to give in to nature rather than see someone else take over a project he began and, I fear, he will resent your working here, regarding you as an intruder and a threat.'

She sighed, at the same time pulling out a packet of cigarettes from her mackintosh pocket and inserting one in her long holder, lighting it with her head cocked to one side like a blackbird listening for a worm.

'He will come round to you in time, though you will have to be patient with him. When he sees the improvement to his rhubarb bed he will unbend a little. Meanwhile,' she repeated, 'you will have to be patient.'

It seemed a strange place, the Hoad Hill Guest House, and I had yet to see a single guest.

og

My parents were unimpressed when I told them I was successful at my interview. I failed to mention I was the sole applicant, and I was evasive about Florence, Doris and Albert. My mother had never heard of the place, which surprised me for she knew most of the goings on within a radius of twenty miles. Doubtless she would make enquiries and soon know more about it than I ever would.

'Don't think you can use my car every day,' she said 'I need it for shopping and for travelling to my bridge parties. You'll have to make your own arrangements for going to this guest house of yours.'

I had already thought of this: fortunately there was an excellent bus service I could use. I hoped, like Albert, she would come round to the idea of my new employment and unbend a little, but her next words left me in little doubt of her feelings.

'If you think you can spend the rest of your life digging a rhubarb bed, after the expensive education we have given you, then you are mistaken. Look at your friends. Most of them are starting good jobs in accountancy and law, using their qualifications and making a start in life whilst the best you can manage is working in an old peoples' home digging a rhubarb bed. Why do they grow so much rhubarb anyway?' I thought the question was best left unanswered.

෨

I started work the next day. My mother had second thoughts about the Morris Minor 'as it was my first day.' Forence showed me to a large garage at the side of the guest house which, to my surprise, was full of ancient dusty cars which evidently had not been driven for some considerable time.

'Park it in there,' she instructed me. 'Don't worry about blocking anyone in, these cars are never used now.' Sensing my curiosity, she went on, 'My guests always bring their cars with them when they come to stay with me, but most of them are far too old and infirm to drive any more. They see their cars as a symbol of their past life, almost as if they could drive back to their independence and younger days, although they know perfectly well this is impossible. I often see them taking furtive looks at their old cars, even dusting them sometimes. Still,' she went on, 'it gives them something to cling to, which is no bad thing, and they pay me good rent for their garage space.'

I went down the garden in search of Doris, passing Albert on the way. I wished him a 'Good Morning' and was rewarded with another grunt. I wondered whether he was capable of coherent speech and was starting to think that single grunt comprised his entire vocabulary. Doris gave me a fork and a wheelbarrow and I started digging the rhubarb bed. It was in a terrible state, covered by invasive weeds of every description: obviously Albert had been unable to cope with it long before his operation and the whole half acre had slipped into a decay of matted weeds. There were weeks of work ahead, and I calculated by the time I had finished I would have to start at the beginning again: it looked like a job for life, though I doubted the thought would have pleased my parents. It was hard work and my slack muscles soon ached, protesting at the unaccustomed strain I was imposing on them. The barrow filled rapidly and I tipped the weeds into a heap at the edge of the plot where Albert, who must have had something of the pyromaniac in him, eagerly ignited them, sending clouds of smoke drifting across to where I was digging. It was, I reflected, wiping my streaming eyes with the back of my hand, his particular revenge on the young intruder invading his territory. I soon learnt to tip the weeds upwind and Albert abandoned his attempts to incinerate them.

At ten o' clock the maid, the same one who had opened the door to me the previous day, brought me a cup of tea and a plate of biscuits. The chipped china was embossed with 'The Hoad Hill Guest House' in ornate lettering. I took my tea break in the greenhouse, where a chair without a back had been thoughtfully provided.

An hour or so later I saw my first guest, a tall well dressed man smoking a pipe and carrying a shooting stick. He slowly made his way down to the edge of the rhubarb bed, carefully pressed his shooting stick into the grass path and sat watching me, wordlessly, smoking his pipe, a smile playing around his lips. He appeared to follow every move I made with interest until, after an hour, he pulled back the cuff of his shirt to consult his watch. He tapped out his pipe on the shaft of his shooting stick, freed it from the ground, folded the handles and made his way back to the house, smiling to himself all the time. He must have been nearly ninety.

Sometimes Doris left her pigs and goats and inspected my work, interested, no doubt, to see how her new employee was faring. She seemed happy enough, remarking the bed was in a worse state than she had thought. At twelve o' clock I ate the sandwiches my mother had made me, sitting in the greenhouse on the hard backless chair.

The maid, whose name was Amy, brought me my afternoon cup of tea at three o' clock, picking her way awkwardly down the path, looking out of place in her starched uniform in the wilderness of the rhubarb bed. She was a thin bony old woman whose severe looks belied her friendly nature and insatiable appetite for gossip. After a while I became friendly with Amy and she supplied me with all the details of life – and, very often, death – at the guest house.

My life settled to a steady routine of digging. The old man with the shooting stick still arrived to watch me at precisely the same time each day, never uttering a word. I wondered how he would cope when it rained.

ဆ

My parents grudgingly accepted their expensively educated son was working as a gardener although they were far from happy with the idea.

'Your mother is worried about you,' my father told me as we played a round of golf one Saturday afternoon. 'She thinks you will be left behind if you don't soon look for a proper job.'

I suspected she was far more worried explaining to her friends in the bridge circle she had joined how her son was working in a menial job, while their sons were taking their first strides in the world of 'The Professions'. I also suspected these friends of hers extracted a perverse and lingering pleasure in extolling the various virtues of their sons, leaving my mother with little defence.

I had no desire to rush into 'a profession', spending my days in air-conditioned offices, attending endless pointless meetings, juggling figures and balancing books: my aptitude for mathematics was minimal in any case. I had just emerged from ten years of monastic boarding school life and I needed time to clear my mind. The Hoad Hill Guest House provided the perfect antidote to private education and, for the moment, I was content.

It was difficult to explain this to my father, but I think he understood. His worry was more with my mother than with me as he explained over a drink in the clubhouse when we had completed our round.

'If you don't think of something soon,' he said, 'your mother will think of something for you.'

೮೮

Doris's perception of Albert proved correct. He progressed from a grunt to a civil 'Good morning' after a couple of weeks and once he realised I was only at the guest house on a temporary basis, became almost loquacious. He was a bachelor and, Doris told me in the manner insiders will confide in outsiders, had harboured designs on Amy for over a quarter of a century. The relationship was doomed for Amy, with her angular sincerity, had told Albert from the start her life was devoted to the care of the elderly.

'She has the single-minded calling of a nun without the need of taking Holy orders.' Doris remarked. 'I think in her declining years she will marry Albert for companionship and nurse him to the grave. She is a remarkable woman.' She looked at me severely. 'Her only vice is gossip, and it is best not to encourage her.'

I encouraged Amy with every effort and she responded readily, divesting the innermost secrets of the guest house, its inhabitants and owners with a charming, innocent naivety.

೮೮

Caponising the chickens comprised one of my 'other duties'; moving furniture and personal effects from departed guests' rooms another. I found both these duties rather gruesome, particularly clearing the rooms. Public school had not prepared me for the greedy acquisitive instincts of the late guests' relatives and friends, arguing with undignified and unseemly fervour in the car park at the rear of the guest house over rights of ownership, watched by bewildered removal men, a confused gardener and Albert. Florence and Doris, wisely, kept out of the way. Doubtless they were well experienced in such uncivilised behaviour. Albert was unmoved.

'They're disgusting,' he told me, observing my expression the first time

14

I witnessed the spectacle. 'They behave like spoilt children fighting over each others' Christmas presents. No wonder the world's in such a mess with people we're supposed to respect carrying on like that, and in forty years time their children will act just the same, you'll see.'

I sincerely hoped I would not be working at the Hoad Hill Guest House, or any other guest house for that matter, in thirty or forty years time to witness such unedifying scenes.

It was scarcely more edifying caponising the chickens or, more correctly, feminising the cockerels to make them heavier and more succulent.

This macabre, unnatural operation took place in the capacious corrugated iron hen-house in a flurry of flying feathers and dust, spiced with the eye-watering stench of ammonia. Albert and I caught the unfortunate fowl and passed them to Doris who, with practised ease, inserted a pellet containing a deadly cocktail of female hormones under the skin high on the neck, dropping the treated birds through a hatch in the wire netting which divided the hen house. She sat on a wooden chair, totally absorbed in her work whilst we supplied her with protesting, squawking, scrabbling, unwilling victims.

God knows what effect this treatment had on the guests – most were probably past caring anyway – but it certainly put me off chicken for the rest of my life. I was rapidly coming to the conclusion Florence and Doris were a couple of tough old birds.

ભ

Tracking down the Admiral was a much more rewarding and interesting 'other duty'. In addition to my silent observer with the shooting stick, I was frequently visited by the Admiral, a charming old man, hopelessly addicted to alchohol. Nearly all the inhabitants of the guest house were widows or widowers, but the Admiral was an exception. He had, Amy explained to me, become too much of a burden on his wife and she could no longer cope with his eccentricities, exacerbated by his remarkable intake of strong drink. The last straw came when his wife, experiencing difficulty flushing the lavatory, lifted the lid of the cistern and discovered a bottle of gin inside. Her subsequent search of the house revealed more bottles of gin reposing in other lavatory cisterns within the house, and several concealed in the base of a grandfather clock. With the help of a tame doctor, and to the relief of both the Admiral and his wife, he was sent to the Hoad Hill Guest House to live out the rest of his days in complete sobriety, denied alchohol totally.

Amy's sympathies were firmly with the Admiral. His wife, she told me, was a dreadful domineering woman who had undoubtedly driven him to drink. His problems only started in earnest when he had retired and, tired of the constant nagging and streams of orders issuing from this demanding woman, had sought solace with his retired friends in the lounge bar of the local pub. He had, however, stayed on there long after his service friends had obediently returned home and, when he was inevitably informed by the landlord he was no longer welcome, had taken to drinking at home. It was at this stage he was consigned to the guest house.

However, The Admiral was a devious old man. His wife had made it clear to Florence he was only to be supplied with soft drinks and, on no account, alchohol. Her conscience satisfied, she returned home to pursue her social life with her errant husband safely and soberly institutionalised. Unknown to his wife, the Admiral had a secret bank account which, with the connivance of Amy, he used for the purchase of his bottles of gin. It was Albert who procured the gin for him, and the old Admiral collected it from Albert's potting shed twice a week.

'It's a shame to deny him his only pleasure in life.' Amy said with sympathy. 'He hasn't much time left, and he might as well make the most of it.'

It was the perfect arrangement. Freed from his awful wife, the Admiral was happy and she, secure in the knowledge her husband was safe in the guest house, was freed from the responsibility of the wreck she had created.

Paradoxically, life at the guest house had moderated his drinking. With his wife out of the way he probably felt less need for the palliative effects of gin and, although Amy told me she was certain Florence knew he continued to indulge his weakness, he became almost a model guest.

His route to Albert's potting shed passed by my rhubarb bed, and he always paused for a chat. I could hear him coming long before I saw him, for he wheezed like a leaky steam engine, small flecks of white foam coming from his lips. He was also addicted to cigars. He was a short man, with an inevitably florid face, beetle-browed, barrel-chested, and he walked like a penguin, stiff-legged, rocking from side to side, his arms held rigid and unmoving about four inches away from the seam of his trousers. His head was thrust back as he appeared to gaze at the sky through his thick-lensed, horn-rimmed glasses, navigating his way towards his gin. He was a delightful old man. Our chat finished, gasping and spluttering, he continued his journey to the potting shed. It was difficult to believe he had once been in command of hundreds of men.

Twice a month he escaped the confines of the guest house and went on a bender. It was no accident these benders coincided with the visits his wife reluctantly paid him. Florence and Doris became panic-stricken, searching the buildings and grounds for him, knowing full well where he was all the time. It was their reluctance to enter a public house which engendered their futile searches, presumably in the vain hope he had conveniently passed out somewhere, combined with the shame of having to admit they had lost a guest from causes other than the natural. Albert was usually delegated to find him.

When Albert was on a fortnight's holiday Florence, whom I normally saw only on a Friday afternoon when she brought me my wage packet, turned to me.

'He likes you,' she said, 'and he won't be any trouble, only make sure you return him here as quickly as possible. His wife's due for her visit in an hour. He will be at The Red Lion, The White Heart or The Wheatsheaf. Do you know where they are?'

I nodded and set off on my task. I found the amiable Admiral in The Wheatsheaf, playing shove ha'penny in the public bar. He bought me a pint of beer, a large pink gin for himself and a round for his friends at the shove ha'penny board.

Fortified for his impending visit, he came with me as meekly as a lamb, strutting along the pavement with his peculiar penguin gait. We returned to the guest house with a quarter-of-an-hour to spare.

I asked my father, a retired naval officer, if he had come across the Admiral in his time, and the reply was instantaneous.

'A brilliant man,' he said, 'with a great tactical brain. But he had a terrible wife.'

ଔ

My silent observer with the shooting stick was called Percy, I learned from Amy. He was a retired bank manager who had scarcely spoken to anyone since the death of his wife some two years before had predicated his arrival at the guest house. Amy was as puzzled as I that he should take such an interest in the new gardener, but he seemed harmless enough. At first it unnerved me to be watched so closely; after a time I became used to Percy, sitting on his shooting stick, smiling and peacefully smoking his pipe. He arrived at exactly eleven o' clock every morning, and left on the stroke of twelve, uprooting his shooting stick and shuffling back towards the house. He startled me one morning when I was digging in the rain, arriving noisily, clad in a full set of oilskins, his head covered by an outsize sou'wester which conveniently shielded his pipe.

A few days later, as he prepared to return to the warmth of the guest house, he changed his mind and, slowly picking his way across the weeds and lines of rhubarb crowns, came towards me. I ceased digging, watching his painful progress, wondering what on earth he was going to do. He stopped

17

in front of me, hesitated for a moment, and said, 'It gives me great pleasure watching you my boy, more pleasure than you will ever know.' He turned and made his way back across the rhubarb bed. They were the only words he ever spoke to me, and I puzzled over them for days.

I mentioned Percy's apparent obsession and his conversation to Doris. 'He had a son of your age who was killed in the war,' she said. 'You are too young to understand the workings of the older mind, but you will understand in time.' She twisted a cigarette into her holder, her head at an angle as she concentrated, her beret flopping slightly to one side. She would have made a wonderful brown owl. She lit the cigarette, inhaling deeply. 'There is a photograph of his son in his room, and he bears more than a passing resemblance to you. Humour him, for he is a sad old man, and remember, you too will be old one day.'

It would have been tactless to have pointed out to Doris that most of the people who ran The Hoad Hill Guest House were older than some of their guests.

I finished digging the rhubarb bed ten days before Christmas and moved down the garden to the main vegetable plot. Percy moved with me and, in companionable silence, I started digging the easier soil of the vegetable garden. The weather broke with a face-stinging, neck-dripping vengeance and Percy abandoned his morning visits; digging became impossible and I helped Albert in the potting shed until conditions improved.

They never did. The rain hammered down mercilessly, beating the earth to a glistening sheen until the sodden ground could absorb no more and rivulets of mud-laden water trickled off the garden, working their way to the river far below, joining the brown waters which carried the nourishment from the fields and gardens way beyond, depositing them on the sea bed in cruel defiance of man's endeavour.

Perversely, I missed Percy. I asked Doris how he was. She assured me he was in good health, at the same time enquiring at my solicitude. It was not a question I could readily answer, and it occured to me that perhaps I was in danger of becoming institutionalised myself.

It was a point my mother was quick to notice.

'It's not good for you, mixing with all those old people,' she told me in her exasperation. 'You will soon become slow thinking and old in your outlook yourself if you don't take care. It's about time you had a proper job.'

 timescale

It poured down, day after day in the first weeks of January, raining from Monday until Friday and, perversely, clearing up for the weekends. Digging was impossible. On the rare fine days in the week the ground was a squelching bog, far too wet to work. I spent my time in the potting shed with Albert, doing all the jobs that had been set aside for rainy days. Soon there had been so many rainy days there were no more jobs left, and it became clear to me unless the weather improved my days at the guest house, like those of all of its inmates, were numbered. Percy appeared to have sensibily hibernated and, apart from Doris, the only person Albert and I saw was the hardy Admiral, sloshing stiff-legged through the mud twice a week to collect his bottles of gin. Even Amy gave up bringing us cups of tea: she could scarcely be blamed.

The turning point in my gardening career came when Doris killed a batch of capons, and Albert and I spent the day plucking and drawing them.

When I unwisely told my mother, she was furious, 'Your father and I spent a fortune on your education,' she informed me, 'and once had high hopes you would follow the family tradition and join the Navy. Instead, you waste your time digging a rhubarb bed, of all things, dragging drunken men out of public houses (I thought it tactless to mention the Admiral's connection with the Navy) and now you are plucking chickens in a filthy potting shed with a disgusting old man who runs after the maids at your guest house.'

I thought her distortion of what I had told her about Albert, and her summary judgement of him unfair, and said as much, but this only served to inflame her even more.

'If he smells like you when he comes home in the evening, I doubt his maids will ever consider him, and no self-respecting girl would consider you, with the job you have and reeking like a hen house. It's still not too late to consider the Navy.' She ended pleadingly.

It was an old argument. Ten years of rigidly enforced discipline at school had left me in no doubt at all the service life was not for me. The only career holding any interest was agriculture but, as my mother pointed out, the family was not 'connected' with farming. Furthermore, she told me, unless one had connections there was little hope of progressing in the world. Since my family's only connection appeared to be with the Navy, a course I had firmly rejected, we had reached stalemate.

'If you can't think of something very soon, we will think of something for you.' She said ominously, 'remember, you are only eighteen, and until you are twenty-one you will do as your father and I say.'

I related all this to Albert the following morning as I gloomily resumed capon plucking.

'Don't worry lad,' he said, 'You've all your life ahead of you.

Something'll turn up. Your old lady'll see to that.'

It was precisely that which worried me.

ɢƨ

It appeared my family was better connected than my mother had led me to believe. Once she had accepted my rejection of the Navy, she cast around and, unknown to me, thought of the game of golf. My father had many golfing partners, one of them being a Mr. Chubb, a farmer whom I had never met, though my father often spoke of him. Mr. Chubb was the manager of a two thousand acre farm – or estate – three miles up the valley from where we lived.

When I returned home one evening from the guest house, I found my parents in a solemn mood. I knew my father had been playing a round of golf with Mr. Chubb that day, but I was unprepared for the consequences of the game. My father and Mr. Chubb had struck a deal. I was to work for him for nine months on trial as a student, without wages, and if my first nine months proved satisfactory, I was to continue for a further nine months, thus completing the eighteen months practical farm experience required for entry to agricultural college.

I had no say in the matter. I was to hand in my notice to Florence the following day and start work for Mr. Chubb the week after, the last week in January.

Florence, I think, was relieved. 'You almost completed your digging,' she said. 'Albert can easily finish it now. We shall miss you.' She chuckled to herself as she lit a cigarette. 'It never was your sort of job here. We have both taken advantage of each other, and I would like to think you have learnt something from your stay.'

I certainly had: I had also learnt there was more to the game of golf than hitting a ball up the middle of the fairway.

ɢƨ

My sister lived and worked in London. She came home most weekends, often bringing with her her current and usually eccentric young man. The weekend before I began work for Mr. Chubb she arrived at the station alone, doubtless to the relief of my parents, but to my disappointment. Her extraordinary choice of male companions, who afforded me endless amusement, were a constant of worry to my mother.

After our Sunday lunch, my parents sat down in front of a blazing coal fire to read the Sunday newspapers. My sister, bored with the lack of company of her own age, suggested a drive in my mother's Morris Minor. I agreed readily, suggesting a trip to Mr. Chubb's farm. I was unsure of the precise location of the farmyard where I was to start work the following day, and the drive was a good opportunity to find it.

It was a dismal drive. The rain had started again, not a heavy rain, rather a penetrating, enveloping stifling rain, leaving the waterlogged fields looking more suited to growing rice than corn. We skirted the deep puddles as we drove along the lanes which bisected the farm, although I had no idea of the boundaries. Miserable cattle and sheep sheltered in the lee of hedgerows, slowly and methodically chewing their cuds, patiently waiting for the rain to cease: it looked like a long wait.

We descended to the floor of the valley and came into the village on the main road, following the river which neatly divided the village in half, the road crossing and re-crossing it on narrow bridges with brick parapets. I had been through the place countless times without observing it properly: now I took a closer look. The essentials were there – a small shop, a pub and a tiny church. There was no school, the population, presumably, not warranting one. Darkness was falling and the lights were on in the farmworkers' cottages, plumes of smoke rose and hung from the chimney stacks in the damp air. A low mist rose slowly from the swollen river. There was not a soul to be seen, nor a sound to be heard, not even the barking of a dog. We turned off the main road and found the farmyard, adjacent to a small bridge over one of the river's carriers. The yard was rectangular, containing empty trailers unsteadily propped with concrete blocks and backed against the buildings which enclosed it. A large cylindrical fuel tank stood by the entrance. Inevitably the farmyard was deserted, apart from a bedraggled cat, gazing defiantly at us from its shelter underneath one of the trailers.

Behind all those tightly closed doors of the farm cottages the farmworkers, whom I was to join on an honorary basis, were probably reading their lurid Sunday newspapers and drinking cups of strong, scalding tea. As we left the damp, sleeping village where the only inhabitant on view was a solitary manky cat, I wondered what on earth my parents had let me in for.

ଔ

21

2.
Penance with the Potatoes

I returned to the rectangular farmyard at half-past seven the next morning, parking my mother's car carefully alongside one of the trailers. In the half light of the overcast January day, I saw there was a transformation from the visit my sister and I had made there so gloomily the day before. The place was alive with the talk of the farmworkers and the gentle throb of tractor engines warming up. A group of about seven men were being addressed by a man of medium height, whose back was turned to me. Other men were busying themselves with their tractors, backing slowly up to the trailers which were now loaded with unfamiliar, arcane collections of gear.

My arrival caused little stir apart from a few covert glances; as a farm student I evidently did not rate highly. I shut the door of the car, the noise attracting the attention of the man talking to the group. He glanced at me, said a few more words to his men, and came over to me.

He shook my hand firmly, introducing himself, unsurprisingly, as Mr. Chubb. We studied each other for a moment and I reflected it was a curious way to start my student days meeting my employer for the first time on the morning I started working for him. He had a round, slightly reddened face, giving him an innocent cherubic appearance. He was immaculately dressed in sports jacket, neatly pressed trousers and carefully knotted tie. On his feet he wore a pair of black Wellington boots which had about three inches of his thick white socks folded down over the tops. His shining silver hair was perfectly groomed, and I judged him to be about sixty-five.

'Sit yourself in my Land Rover,' he told me, 'and I will show you the farm. First I have to see Fred in his feed mill.'

He vanished through the dark doorway of a two-storeyed building which occupied one end of the farmyard, the front of which was white with dampened dust. I could just see a single feeble light bulb, hanging from a long flex, dimly illuminating the interior.

From my high seat in the Land Rover, I looked around. Most of the men had dispersed, and I took a closer look. Opposite the feed mill was a large barn, the original thatched roof replaced with grey-painted corrugated iron. From the activity I had seen when I arrived, accompanied by billows of diesel smoke pouring out of it, I assumed it was the barn which housed the tractors. The other two sides, the long sides, were bounded by low buildings which housed farm implements of every description. They looked as though they were converted stables, and I discovered later that was exactly their old function, a legacy from the days when the farm was worked by horses rather than the mechanical horse-power housed in the barn.

A tremendous clattering roar of uncoordinated machinery came from the feed mill, starting slowly and increasing in volume until it reached a crescendo, threatening to shake the building down. Suddenly it quietened as the machinery harmonised itself, settling to a steady, powerful rhythm. Clouds of dust, like urban fog, seeped from the door and windows.

Mr. Chubb hastily returned to his Land Rover. I caught a brief glance of a short figure clad in a whitened boiler suit through the solitary doorway.

'Wonderful man, Fred.' said Mr. Chubb. 'He's been with me for over thirty years.' He leant over the steering wheel. 'I will tell you what I will do with you. I always drive round the farm before I take my breakfast, and you can come with me. The drive will give you an idea of the extent of the estate, and then I'll drop you off at the 'tater field.

He pressed the starter of the Land Rover; it was in gear, and lurched forward. Undeterred, he tried again, and we successfully left the farmyard. His concentration was firmly centred on the farm, the fields, the crops and the cattle and sheep which, even to my inexperienced eye, looked magnificent. Driving was a secondary consideration. He randomly groped around for gears – any one sufficed as long as the Land Rover kept moving – spending his time gazing out of the windows, talking half to himself and half to me.

'Marvellous bunch of heifers,' he said, violently correcting the steering with one hand to avoid the bank, the other hand pointing out of the sliding window from which he had been watching. 'The best I have ever reared on this farm.'

Sometimes he stopped the Land Rover, half climbing out before he realised he had neglected to apply the handbrake, twisting round to pull it up, swinging his legs out, wandering off, opening a heavy oak gate to inspect his crops, forgetting I was with him. At one point he suddenly stopped the Land Rover in the middle of the lane for no apparent reason and, with one hand on the knob of the long gear-lever, the other tapping the rim of the steering wheel, turned to me.

'Now listen to me,' he said, suddenly gripping the wheel with both hands and swivelling to face me, 'I told your father I would pay you no wage. Well, I have changed my mind. I shall pay you one pound per week, and you can collect your money from the Major, along with the other men on Friday afternoons,' (the Major, I discovered later, was the farm secretary). 'Secondly, I think it would be best if you took lunch with my wife and myself each Monday. That way I can keep in touch with your progress and you can ask me any questions about technical matters you do not understand. My last student never once asked me a question,' he added darkly, 'and I think it was a mistake not to involve myself more with him.'

The Land Rover jumped forward as he released the clutch and we resumed our tour, Mr. Chubb looking left and right all the time, but seldom at the road.

We followed the lanes my sister and I had travelled the previous afternoon, Mr. Chubb charging through the puddles with reckless abandon. A weak January sun was struggling to burn through the covering of cloud. I had little idea of judging area and was surprised how much land two thousand acres encompassed, from the small water meadows with the chalk stream slowly meandering through to the high, steep downlands two miles away on the far boundary, growing huge fields of winter corn.

'Marvellous land here,' Mr. Chubb remarked, 'it can stand any amount of rain: the chalk takes it all away.'

It was a different picture in the potato field where our tour ended. The Land Rover slithered through the deeply rutted gateway, Mr. Chubb wrestling with the steering wheel as the thick clinging alluvial mud, splattering noisily underneath the wings, made a mockery of his attempts to drive a straight line. He parked next to an older Land Rover, disgracefully dirty, the canvas tilt sagging on its hooped supports and covered with a growth of algae.

Mr. Chubb noticed my glance and grunted. 'That belongs to James,' he said, 'my assistant manager. I will introduce you to him, then I shall be away for my breakfast.'

I shook hands with James, a small sharp-featured man of about twenty-eight. Mr. Chubb departed for his breakfast and I followed James through the soft mud to a tractor and trailer which a number of men were loading with sacks of potatoes.

'We don't normally harvest potatoes in January,' James told me wryly. 'The weather has been so dreadful this winter we have hardly been able to do anything. This,' he said, describing an arc with his arm, 'is a clear up job before the slugs eat what is left of the potatoes. We'll finish the field today, whether it rains or not, and then,' he added ominously, 'we can finish riddling the crop and prepare the field for spring corn.'

The field was swarming with people. The regular farmworkers were supplemented by decrepit and vociferous women, gypsies and itinerant Irishmen who had arrived early for the sugar beet hoeing in the hope of gaining casual work. They were all picking wet, muddy potatoes which had been brought to the surface by the potato lifter, transferring them from galvanised buckets to hessian sacks which stood upright in the field like monoliths, patiently awaiting collection. I helped load these sacks high onto a huge trailer towed, incongrously, behind a Ferguson 35 petrol-engined tractor. The trailer seemed dangerously overloaded.

Few people spoke to me, though a tall man with twinkling blue eyes took a fatherly interest; some of the old women cast aspertions on my virility in coarse, vulgar asides, cackling with laughter at their own humour, not once pausing in their work. It was all a far cry from The Hoad Guest House.

⬉

At twelve o' clock all work ceased for lunch, or dinner as it was termed by the farmworkers. They returned home, together with the women and several elderly men, who were the estate's pensioners. The gypsies and the Irishmen boiled up their kettles with wood gleaned from the hedgerows, baking potatoes in the hot ash.

I drove the short distance down the valley to my home where my mother, determined to make a success of her son's embryonic farming career, had cooked a banquet.

Towards the end of the afternoon, with the trailer loaded with sacks of potatoes almost to the height of a double-decker bus, James suddenly said to me, 'Hop in and move up to the next stack of bags.'

I surveyed the bewildering range of gears, and asked James which one to use.

'Any one you like,' he replied, 'so long as it is not top.'

Selecting a middle range gear, with one half turn of the rear wheels the tractor slowly subsided to its underbelly in the mud. It was, I thought, hardly an auspicious start.

The following day Mr. Chubb sent me to the potato shed – a long, low wide building about half a mile from the farm. Surprisingly, the only farmworkers present were Henry, the relief cowman, an inoffensive man of about fifty-five and a young man called Len, who worked for Mr. Chubb on a casual basis. He lived in the next village, a mile further up the valley. The rest of the gang comprised four of the didicoys I had noticed in the potato field the day before. Presumably the regular farmworkers were employed on more important tasks than riddling potatoes.

We uncovered the potatoes which were layered with straw to protect them from the frost, and pushed the riddler into position. I looked with awe at the riddler: it was a monstrous machine, mounted on iron wheels, constructed mostly of wood. It looked like something from the middle ages. The potatoes were shovelled into a small hopper, from where they ascended a set of wooden rollers, bumping and jostling, shedding their dirt before dropping onto a sieve placed on the centrepiece of the machine. This was a large box which shook mesmerically back and forth, the potatoes shedding yet more dirt, the smaller ones dropping through the sieve and the larger ones working their way across to another set of rollers, completing their journey by falling into paper sacks placed at the end. There were cunningly situated chutes and holes through which reject potatoes irregularly exited into buckets standing around the sides. The machine was powered by a noisy petrol engine, which precluded all conversation.

It required an enormous amount of maintenance. Periodically we shut the machine off, the welcome freedom from the roar of the engine replaced with the tedium of scraping compacted mud off the rollers, clearing the dirt from underneath, cleaning the sieves, greasing the chains and the countless grease nipples scattered from one end of the riddler to the other.

It was thoroughly boring work, and to make matters worse the long sliding doors to the shed had to be left wide open to disperse the fumes from the petrol engine, introducing an Arctic blast of air which chilled us to the marrow. The most sought after job was shovelling the potatoes into the hungry jaws of the riddler: it was the only way to keep warm. The rest of us stood, frozen, around the machine picking off damaged and reject potatoes and throwing them into bags which were streched open across tall holders.

Len kept a supply of bags where the stitching had rotted out from the bottoms. Whenever Henry's bag of rotten potatoes was full, he swung it off the bag holder only to find all the potatoes deposited in a clammy mess on the floor. Len solicitiously helped Henry pick them up and carefully placed another bottomless bag on the holder. It was an endless performance which Henry never had the wit to query, and it was a measure of our boredom we found it so amusing.

The only respites from the tedium of riddling were the arrival of a lorry to collect the bagged potatoes, or a breakdown, both of which were eagerly awaited. Unfortunately, the riddler rarely obliged, though it was usually spectacular when it occured, and loading the lorry was extended as far as was decently possible.

I found any relief from the silence of the engine as trying as the riddling itself. The didicoys, for reasons I found difficult to understand, found me inescapably fascinating and besieged me with questions at every opportunity. As a farm student I evidently exercised a certain novelty value for them and they were determined to make the most of it. It was my misfortune to find them totally incomprehensible – they might have been speaking Chinese for all I knew – firing questions at me with frightening speed. I felt I needed an interpreter, and Len and Henry were no help, talking to each other, professing an equal ignorance of the didicoys' obscure dailect as my own. I didn't believe them for a minute, suspecting they kept themselves apart from the men from the smoky country simply because of a traditional irrational fear and dislike farmworkers had of gypsies. Consequently I had their undivided attention, and soon learnt to answer 'yes' on 'no' according to their tone of voice. Answering in the affirmative to what turned out to be a question regarding my age must have left them in some doubt as to the quality of farm students, but they were a friendly family for, in the way of gypsies, they were all related and all bore the same surname – Brazil.

'And they'se all nuts too,' Len informed me after they had gone home in their rickety old truck. 'I never 'as liked didicoys, they'se clannish and evil.'

                       ೞ

Mr. Chubb paid us occasional brief visits but apart from impressing upon everyone smoking was strictly forbidden – on account of the readily combustible straw – seldom lingered. Needless to say, this edict was flagrantly ignored and it never ceased to amaze me how the riddling gang – all of whom smoked incessantly – possessed a sixth sense which accurately predicted the times of his arrival. Cigarettes were suddenly and wordlessly extinguished and within ten minutes Mr. Chubb's Land Rover would appear by the door. It was not as if his visiting times were regular, nor could the engine of his Land Rover be heard above the roar of the riddler, but everyone knew just when he was coming.

                       ೞ

At the end of my first Friday afternoon, after the potatoes had been covered down with straw, using long-handled pitchforks – or two-grained prongs as Henry termed them – we locked the shed, concealing the key under a large concrete block, and made our way to the farm office to collect our wages. A ragged queue of scruffy men waited by the door, talking cheerfully, scuffing their feet on the ground – some wore black Wellingtons, others hobnailed boots – smoking their cigarettes and frequently spitting onto the concrete path. They all had Army surplus haversacks which contained their lunch boxes, slung over their shoulders, the tops of their thermos flasks showing through the edges of the canvas covers. We joined the end of the queue and the men fell silent, looking furtively round at us. It was, I hoped, the arrival of the didicoys and not that of the student which caused the silence. The door to the farm office remained firmly closed, while we waited in the queue.

The office door opened, and we shuffled forwards. I was surprised to see James in the queue; apparently on pay day he was treated as a farm worker rather than assistant manager. The men came out, some thrusting their brown pay packets into their pockets, others checking the contents under the porch light in the half darkness of the late January afternoon. I entered the office in my turn. The Major, impeccably dressed, sitting behind his desk, his wavy white hair carefully groomed, handed me my pay packet containing one pound, ticking my name off on a list with a silver propelling pencil. Mr. Chubb was standing beside him. He beamed at me.

'I'm away to a golf tournament tomorrow, he said, 'so I'll not be seeing you. Don't forget you are having lunch with Mrs. Chubb and myself Monday. Half past twelve, prompt.

The Major looked up. 'Knowing Mrs. Chubb's cooking as I do,' he said, 'I doubt you'll be any use in the potato shed afterwards.'

Mr. Chubb beamed with pleasure.

cs

I knocked on Mr. Chubb's door at half past twelve, prompt, on Monday afternoon. The fact that 'dinner' started on the farm at twelve and finished at one had evidently not occured to him, but at least it shortened my time in the dreadful potato shed. It had not escaped Len's notice, though, and he grumbled all morning at the way the student was shown special favours while everyone else did the work. 'You'll not learn farming having dinner with Mr. Chubb,' he said. 'Your place is 'ere, in the 'tater shed with us.'

Mr. Chubb opened the door and courteously showed me to the cloakroom. 'Leave your boots on the mat,' he said, 'I'll find you a pair of my old slippers while you wash your hands.'

He took me through to the kitchen where he introduced me to Mrs. Chubb, a small dark-haired woman who must have been astonishingly attractive when she was younger. Now in her middle sixties, working in a steaming kitchen, a curl of her hair engagingly sticking to her temple where she had brushed an arm across to remove it from her eyes, she retained most of the good looks of her youth. We shook hands, and Mr. Chubb led me through to the drawing room.

'Sit down over there,' he said, vaguely indicating a number of armchairs, 'and I'll make us a cocktail.'

I sat and watched him. He opened bottles from his cocktail cabinet apparently at random, pouring small measures into our glasses, pausing, selecting another bottle, adding a little more until he was satisfied. He topped the glasses with tonic water, added some ice, and handed me mine, saying 'Try that,' and, almost before I could take a sip, asking 'What do you think of it?'

It was a difficult question to answer as beer was the only alcoholic drink my parents allowed me and I was no connoisseur of the finer points of exotic cocktails. It certainly tasted powerful.

'I thought you would like it,' he said before I could reply, sinking deeply into his chair, resting his slippered feet on a footstool. 'Mrs Chubb won't touch them,' he continued, 'she says they make her feel lightheaded.'

It was something I could well understand.

He smiled. 'You have proved a worry to your mother and father,' he went on, 'digging that rhubarb bed in the old folks' home. I don't think your father minded too much, but I gather your mother took a dim view of it.' He leant forward in his chair, his drink in his hand. 'I will tell you this,' he said, casting a quick glance towards the kitchen, 'It is the women you have to watch; they run the world. You'll find that out when you are older.'

He eased himself back into his chair. 'How are you getting on in the 'tater shed?' he asked. I replied, as tactfully as I could manage, that I thought the work repetitive and found the didicoys difficult to understand.

'Wonderful family, the Brazils,' he said. 'They have been coming to me for years, although I have never seen these ones before. They are such a large family it is not possible to know them all, but I have known old Henry Brazil for years and he always sends me some of his family when I need them.'

29

He paused. 'A difficult man to understand,' he said. 'I only ever catch half of what he says. You will soon settle in here and get to know my men.' he continued, draining his glass and looking at his watch. 'I do believe we have time for another drink before lunch.'

Mrs. Chubb joined us for a brief glass of sherry before serving lunch, which was all the Major had led me to expect. Midway through, Mr. Chubb suddenly pointed his fork at me. 'I hear you play golf,' he said. We must play a round sometime and perhaps include James. He is a fine golfer and a fine cricketer, too, wasting his talents working here.' (It was always one of my regrets that in all the time I knew Mr. Chubb the projected game of golf never took place.)

When lunch was completed and my offer to help clear the table politely and firmly refused, Mr. Chubb came with me to the back door. 'Put the slippers where you found them,' he said, 'and you can use them when you come next Monday.'

He looked at his watch. It was half past two. 'You had best get back to the 'tater shed,' he said, 'or that Len will be cross. I don't like Len,' he went on darkly. 'I think I might give him the sack.'

○ℰ

He was right. Back at the potato shed Len was furious, leaving me in little doubt of his feelings towards the student. The didicoys were delighted with his performance, passing loud and incomprehensible asides to me for the remainder of the afternoon: Henry stoically removed the rotten potatoes from the riddler, throwing them into the bottomless bags without passing any comment. When we locked the shed at the end of the day, and with Len out of earshot, he said to me, 'Don't take no notice of Len. 'Ee ain't even one of us, an' 'ee'll soon be gone. It ain't 'ardly your fault you was late back, an' that Len thinks 'ee's something 'ee ain't. If the rest of us were 'ere 'ee wouldn't be so cocky.'

I drove the old Morris Minor home, thinking about the day, suddenly realising the subject of farming had never once been raised at lunchtime.

○ℰ

I spent six unbroken weeks riddling potatoes, and I was beginning to wonder whether this was a form of penance for getting the tractor stuck on my first day, some sort of student exploitation or, more likely, a test of my resolve, when Mr. Chubb decided I had learnt enough of this particular purgatory, and moved me on to the spring sowing.

I never did understand the didicoys.

○ℰ

30

3.
Spring Sowing and Lambing

Mr. Chubb was correct: I was coming to know the men better, but it was a slow process. I met them in the farmyard each morning before leaving for the potato shed, and I met them outside the farm office on Friday afternoons when we were paid. Mostly it was a nod, or a brief 'Good morning'. I felt at a disadvantage, for the previous farm student had his roots closer to the farm workers than I, and there were times when I felt as distanced from them as the didicoys.

The spring sowing, which was well advanced by now, brought me into closer contact with Mr. Chubb's men. My sojourn in the potato shed had precluded me from the everyday farm work; there was a lot of ground to make up, none more so than getting to know these men I was to work with for the rest of my time on the estate.

'I am sending you discing,' Mr. Chubb said on my first morning of freedom from the drudgery of the potatoes. 'James will sort you out. You can drive the Ferguson.'

I was reunited with the same Ferguson on which I had made such a brief debut as a tractor driver, and James walked from the barn carrying two rusty lengths of metal. I had no idea what Mr. Chubb meant by 'discing', but had learnt by now to bide my time, knowing the intricacies of discing would be revealed without further enquiry.

James knelt at the rear of the tractor and began fitting the lengths of metal to the hydraulic lift arms. They were, he explained, stabiliser bars which prevented excessive swing. He took one off, looked at it for a moment before replacing it the other way round.

'It's years since we used the Ferguson for cultivation,' he said, 'and my memory is as rusty as these bars. Mr. Chubb,' he went on with unconscious irony, 'thought it best you used the Ferguson as it's such a forgiving tractor.'

He pushed the final clip into position and stood up. 'Back onto the discs,' he said, indicating a set of disc-harrows parked at the back of the farmyard. I tentatively reversed the Ferguson up to them and James connected the harrows to the three-point linkage, working with quick, bird-like movements.

'Now, take it up to the field, and I'll meet you there and start you off.'

Soon I was happily driving up and down the field, glancing behind, watching the disc harrows reducing the rough earth to a pleasing tilth.

Mr. Chubb was adept at dispensing advice, some outrageous, some practical and some so obtuse I had difficulty understanding it. During our weekly lunches I was swamped with his philosophy while Mrs. Chubb, who had heard it all many times before, silently picked at her food. 'When you get married, remember you have to look at the same face over the breakfast table for the rest of your life.' Mrs. Chubb gave a tired smile to that one. 'You had better make a success of this or we are all wasting our time.' His previous student had ended up running a laundry and Mr. Chubb had never forgiven him – and 'Never tell a man to do a job you cannot do your self.'

I had cause to remember this last piece of advice when Mr. Chubb drove into the field an hour later. He inspected my work, poking the earth with his stick, walking up and down the freshly harrowed field, a frown on his face. I watched him anxiously, eager to please, at the same time suspecting Mr. Chubb had found fault.

As I passed close to him he suddenly pulled his handkerchief from his top pocket and waved it from side to side over his head. I took this to be a signal to stop, and switched off the Ferguson.

'This will not do at all,' he said, 'these discs are set all wrong. Come off the tractor and I will show you how to do the job properly.'

He thrust his stick at me with an abrupt 'Hold that' and climbed aboard the Ferguson. He surveyed the controls and turned the key. Nothing happened.

'How do you start this thing?' he asked.

'With the gear lever in neutral.' I replied. He grunted, started the tractor and made a pass up the field.

'You see what I mean,' he said, 'these discs are not doing a thing.'

'How do you adjust them?'

It was too much to have hoped Mr. Chubb was learning too.

Mr. Chubb's idiosyncratic handkerchief waving in moments of crisis was ignored by the farmworkers but, as the student, I felt it my duty to discover his requirements, which were generally exactly those which I intended to carry out in the first place. Many months later, in the middle of harvest, with the dryer overflowing with corn, I was taking my full trailer to park it under cover and collect a spare empty trailer to take back to the harvest field. Out of the corner of my eye I saw Mr. Chubb frenetically waving his handkerchief. I stopped, turned round and drove up the steep hill to the dryer, like a moth drawn to a candle.

'Why have you come up here?' he asked.

'Because you were waving your handkerchief, Mr. Chubb,' I replied. He shook his head slowly from side to side in silent admonition. 'You should know by now when I wave my handkerchief what you have to do. I was only trying to tell you to leave your full trailer in the barn and collect an empty one to take back to the field. There was no need to come all the way up here.'

I gave up then, ignoring his handkerchief waving like everyone else.

൦ള

The farming day started at seven-thirty when Mr. Chubb issued his orders in the farmyard to the assembled workers. They were all well used to his ways and hardly needed telling what to do. They had spent years on the farm – many had been born and brought up in the village – and one rotation followed another with a regular inevitability, hardly changing over the decades.

For me, it was all a new experience and I found Mr. Chubb's orders confusing and contradictory. At times he assumed I had a lifetime's experience in farming, naming implements to hitch onto my tractor that I had never heard of, and often instructing me to take my Ferguson to places I did not know existed, marching into the feed mill before I had the opportunity to question him.

Far worse was his misuse of field names. Every field had a name and I prided myself in knowing most of them, although I had only been on the farm for a relatively short time. His eccentric way with these names baffled me in the same way as his handkerchief waving had so confounded me, for he transposed the names, telling me to go to one field but meaning another, often miles away and called something completely different.

The old hands knew all Mr. Chubb's nuances, but they were not going to enlighten me; it was something I would have to find out for myself, and they listened with scarcely concealed delight when Mr. Chubb told me in the farmyard one morning to take a load of seed corn and fertiliser to Windens. I loaded the trailer and innocently drove to the field; it was deserted and, besides, it was a grass ley. Puzzled, I looked around and saw Mr. Chubb's Land Rover parked by the headland. He walked over to me, his hands thrust deep into his trouser pockets.

'What are you doing up here?' he enquired.

'It's where you told me to go, Mr. Chubb.' I replied.

He sighed deeply. 'You should know by now when I say one field I mean another,' he explained patiently. 'I wanted you to take your load to Long Field, down by the old long barn. You had best hurry, they will be waiting for you.'

I suspected it was no coincidence Mr. Chubb had arrived so precipitately at Windens, and doubtless my misinterpretation of his orders afforded the farmworkers vast amusement: it was, after all, part of the fun of having a farm student in their midst and they could hardly be blamed for reaping the maximum advantage from it.

I had, however, learnt my lesson. In the mornings I would patiently and uncomprehendingly listen to Mr. Chubb's orders and, when he had departed, take the easy way out, asking someone else what he really meant.

ை

One of my many tasks during the sowing was harrowing behind the drill. Harry, the tractor driver, an unbelievably ugly man of about sixty, normally a man of few words, forcibly and eloquently told me if I harrowed out his wheel mark there would be little point in continuing my farming career: harrowing out the drill's wheel mark was as big a sin as one could commit at sowing time, for it meant the tractor driver had no line to follow. Far more than that, there was professional pride at stake, for when the corn emerged the misses between the passes were plain for all to see, right through to harvest time and beyond. It was always the tractor driver in charge of the drill who had to endure almost daily taunts, until the winter ploughing mercifully eradicated the evidence of a moment's lapse in concentration; it was no use blaming the student, he was not in charge of the drill.

'If you 'arrows out my wheel mark,' Harry concluded, dramatically shaking his fist next to my face, 'I'll 'it yer.' It was difficult to know whether he was serious, but a closer look at the staring eyes behind his flat-lensed, tight-fitting, wire-framed glasses convinced me he was.

ை

The spring sowing was almost over and had passed off nearly without incident, but not quite. The drilling team consisted of two men – Harry, driving the tractor, and Frank, the man who tended the drill, standing on a narrow wooden step which ran the length of the machine, sometimes hanging on like grim death on the steeper ground, leaning across the drill grabbing a handhold like a sidecar passenger balancing a motorcycle combination in a race. His job was to ensure the corn and fertiliser ran smoothly down the tubes without blocking.

Frank was a tall, immensely strong man, no more than thirty-five, unusual on the farm as a relatively young man who did not hold a driving licence; mostly it was the older hands who had never driven a tractor.

Mr. Chubb liked to ride on the back of the drill when he visited the field, to Frank's annoyance, and he sometimes remained there for half an hour or more. He maintained it gave him the atmosphere of the operation, and he stood there – silent, bumping up and down the field with horizontal tears from the cold wind streaming across his face, his extinguished pipe held firmly between his teeth.

One day, as the tractor approached the headland nearest to his Land Rover, he jumped off the drill, forgetting the small set of harrows it trailed behind, becoming inexorably enmeshed in them. The tractor completed its turn and started up the field again trailing the drill, Frank, standing on the step and Mr. Chubb, prostrate in the harrows.

Unfortunately for Mr. Chubb, Harry was probably reliving the Normandy landings – he was inclined to live in a world of his own to the exclusion of everything else – and despite the frantic yells from Frank and the furious and unrepeatable expletives from Mr. Chubb in the harrows, it was some hundred yards before Harry realised anything was amiss.

Apart from his pride and a few bruises, Mr. Chubb was, amazingly, unhurt. He sacked Harry and Frank on the spot and limped off to his Land Rover. The drilling team continued with their work: they knew Mr. Chubb better than he knew himself.

♋

Most of the Fordson Majors had flimsy canvas cabs, offering some protection from the wind and rain. My Ferguson 35 was bereft of any such adornment and, following the drill with the drag harrows when the east wind screeching off the downs, dipping relentlessly and unheeding into the valley, the cold was almost paralysing, welding body and mind into a common hatred of its origins.

A peck of dust might well be worth a King's ransom to a farmer in March, but to a frozen farm student swaddled in layers of sweaters, driving a cabless tractor on the steep downland, this peck turned to billows of the stuff, driven by the merciless wind howling unchecked from the wastelands of Northern Siberia. The wind was no respecter of clothing and the relative inactivity of driving a tractor combined with the wind and the dust made harrowing a miserable, icy drudgery. As I passed close to the drill, Frank stepped off and came towards me. His face was streaked with crusted brown dust and a huge dewdrop hung wobbling unsteadily at the end of his nose. He removed his gloves and handed them to me.

' 'Ere, nipper, I reckons you needs these more 'n I.'

He turned and walked back to the drill.

♋

My protracted Monday lunches with Mr. Chubb were both a source of amusement and frustration to the farmworkers, the former prompting ribald conjecture and the latter annoyance when I returned late to whatever job I had been carrying out beforehand. It was useless to point out I was only earning one eighth of a farmworker's wage, or that I had no control over the length of these lunches. The reply was always the same: you are here to learn farming, and you won't learn farming drinking Mr. Chubb's strong cocktails and returning half way through the afternoon barely fit to work.

In one respect they were right. These lunches were supposed to be my opportunity to talk farming with Mr. Chubb, but it seldom turned out to be the case. Mr. Chubb, I discovered, had a voracious appetite for gossip and scandal, and we had a certain common ground as he knew many of my parents' friends and acquaintances. Emboldened by the powerful concoctions, and prompted by Mr. Chubb I became reckless in the information I divulged and, later, almost desperate as my supply of information exhausted itself. My parents must have wondered at the sudden interest their son showed in their friends. I had trapped myself on a treadmill of supply.

At the conclusion of one of these lunches, as I was removing Mr. Chubb's worn out slippers by the back door he said, almost as an afterthought, 'I am sending you to the lambing pens tomorrow. We had our first lambs a couple of days back, and Alan could do with some help. He is a good boy, very conscientious, hard-working and enthusiastic. He has only been with me for a short time,' he added, 'and he is still feeling his way. You will get on well.'

☙

Mr. Chubb's conception of time left much to be desired. Alan, who was the same age as Frank almost to the day, had worked on the farm for over ten years. A slight, softly spoken man with a sunken face which blossomed into rounded good looks on the rare occasions he inserted his false teeth, Alan was the farm's notional shepherd.

The estate's flock of two hundred and fifty Suffolk cross ewes occupied a back seat in the farming rotation. They were really an anachronism from the days when sheep were used as a mobile means of fertilising the fields before the advent of artificial fertiliser, and lambs and wool were secondary to the main purpose of the flock. Mr. Chubb, whose primary interests were corn and cattle, was a traditionalist and insisted the farm maintained a small flock to fit in with, and supplement, the rotation; the sheep were thus undergoing an uneasy transition from their relatively passive role as soil enrichers to the more profitable production of lambs and wool. The farm lagged far behind the specialist sheep farmers and it was difficult to justify Alan as a full-time shepherd other than at lambing time.

''Ee keeps saying 'ee's going to increase the flock,' Alan told me sadly, 'but 'ee never does. It's as if 'ee don't know whether 'ee wants to keep sheep or not.'

The lambing pens lay in the bowl of a vast natural amphitheatre of steep uncultivated downland, reached by a rough track about a mile long which looped up the side of a hill, down through a bluebell wood and emerged startlingly into one of the most beautiful, unspoilt and unknown vistas in the county. It was like entering a new world, a world unchanged for centuries. As the trees thinned and the vivid colours of the bluebells faded behind, the peace became soporific, broken only by the singing of the birds or the call of a ewe to her lamb. Time had no place in this idyllic setting; far from any roads and houses, it was the very timelessness of it that conjured images of countless generations of farm labourers setting about their work, untroubled and in perfect harmony with themselves and their enchanting surroundings.

This peace and the beauty were wasted on Alan. He was too intense and lost within himself to notice them, his mind fixed firmly on other matters. He enjoyed the facility of an enquiring mind and a photographic memory without the means to understand either. An astute salesman had sold him the entire set of *Encyclopaedia Britannica* on the never-never and his relaxation was indulging himself in these volumes, shutting out all other thoughts, excepting those related to his beloved sheep. He could accurately quote paragraphs from the encyclopaedia to me without understanding a word of what he had read, and then ask me to explain. He read these encyclopaedias like novels, digesting their contents and remembering every word, determined to obtain value for his money. He was a mine of useless information and obscure facts which meant nothing to him and very little to anyone else. The theory of gravity completely defeated him, and I spent hours patiently explaining how the inhabitants of the antipodes were able to walk around in the same manner in the southern hemisphere as we managed in the northern counterpart, even demonstrating with the apple he invariably brought with him in his lunch box. It was hopeless.

'I just doesn't see 'ow they stays upright,' he said, with a touching naivety and perfect sincerity. It was an interesting statement, and one to which I could find no convincing answer.

Alan was reputed to have marital problems, which went a long way to explaining his seeking solace in the pages of *Encyclopaedia Britannica*. He led a solitary life at lambing time – at other times he was as much a general farmworker as the others until the sheep required attention – and, I think, he welcomed me helping him with the lambing when, as an outsider, he could confide his thoughts in a way he would never have dared with his more mentally agile colleagues who were more ready than I to pounce on his inadequacies.

37

He made up for his lack of intelligence with a genuine enthusiasm for his sheep, and where I had failed so abjectly in explaining gravity to him, he proved, unconsciously, a much better teacher and it was this infectious enthusiasm which sowed the seed of my lifetime interest in sheep.

We had an unvarying routine for the lambing – Alan's routine – feeding the ewes first thing in the morning before dealing with the crop of lambs born during the night. The newly-born lambs, with their mothers, were placed in individual pens constructed from wheat straw with sheets of corrugated iron, weighted down with further bales, covering the rear as protection from the weather. After we had attended to the lambs, Alan tipped each ewe onto her back to test her milk, at the same time checking her feet and worming her. Foot-rot was prevalent on the farm, and Alan carefully pared their feet with his knife, spraying the affected areas with the gentian violet foot-rot spray when he had completed his work.

'I 'ates these things,' he said, slowly turning the aerosol tin around until the arrow on the nozzle pointed directly into his face. 'They always puts the arrow the wrong way up.'

Pressing the nozzle, the violet spray hissed into his face causing Alan to leap back, wiping the sleeve of his boiler suit over his eyes, spreading the dripping liquid over his brow, nose, cheeks and chin, where it dried, penetrating the skin, defying all attempts to remove it with soap and water.

He could be spotted from afar at lambing time, happily glowing bright purple as if he had been on an almighty bender, his hands matching the curious discoloration of his complexion.

೧

There was one small but very black cloud that darkened the horizon of an otherwise perfect introduction to lambing: it was Cyril.

Cyril was a boy of about seven and he was, without doubt, the most obnoxious, accident-prone nuisance I have ever come across, either before or since. He was a child without one single redeeming feature. He lived in a house at the very beginning of the track leading to the lambing pens, which was unfortunate as I drove directly to the field each morning rather than calling into the farmyard. He waylaid me nearly every day, demanding a lift. If I refused, he started sobbing, his shoulders heaving silently at first, tears pouring down his cheeks, his blurred eyes looking pleadingly into mine. As I prepared to move off, he put his head back and gave vent to a startlingly hideous unbroken bout of screams which must have been audible miles away. Terrified his mother would hear I hastily relented, flinging open the passenger door which I had craftily locked beforehand, and Cyril, instantly cured of his tantrum, sat beside me in smug silence. In stronger moments I sped determinedly past him, but the result was the same for Cyril walked up to the field.

'Why don't that bloody nipper go to school like the rest and leave us in peace?' asked Alan. ' 'Ee's a bloody pest. I 'ates to think what 'ee'll be like when 'ee's older.'

I could well imagine, and I suspected his teachers were delighted at his truancy, leaving Alan and me to suffer the attentions of this dreadful child.

Alan was a mild-mannered man, not given to the inevitable expletives which punctuated every sentence the other farmworkers spoke, but Cyril revealed a vocabulary I never suspected within Alan. Normally placid, he resorted to cuffing Cyril on the head, but nothing deterred him. We forcibly sent him home in the morning, only to have him return in the afternoon: there was no respite from Cyril. On the very few occasions we were not plagued by him, it was as if someone had ceased using a pneumatic drill, a noise which had become so much part of the day we were conditioned to it; the ensuing silence, puzzling at first, suddenly reminding us of the fragility of the peace we had formerly taken for granted, and knowing at any time it could be broken. On these days we cast nervous glances over our shoulders towards the distant gate at the entrance to the field, looking for a small figure determinedly making its way towards us. Sometimes we enjoyed a Cyril-free day, but more often than not our glances revealed the awful Cyril and we knew our day was doomed.

With all the sympathy engendered for what are now fashionably termed single parent families, Cyril was a disaster and sympathy evaporated like early mist on a hot summer morning.

He dropped buckets of water over freshly bedded pens, he cut himself on lambsfoot knives and bled copiously, dripping blood abandonedly over Alan's lunch box and flask. 'I didn't know a nipper of 'is size 'ad so much blood in 'im,' Alan once remarked. He fell into the water troughs, emerging screaming and soaked, protesting violently when we heartlessly made him walk home to change, he lost vital lambing equipment: in short, he nearly drove us mad. And all the time he talked unceasingly, in a high-pitched nasal whine which compounded the irritation of his character. If there was a worse child in the world than Cyril, I have yet to meet him.

'Why are you not at school, boy?' Mr. Chubb asked him on one of his visits to the lambing field.

'I got a cold, mister,' he replied, snivelling convincingly.

'A cold never prevented me from attending school,' said Mr. Chubb. Cyril smiled slyly. I wished his immersions in the water troughs would bring on pneumonia, but it was a forlorn hope: Cyril was too hardy a child to succumb to such an ailment.

ᖳ

Sheep have perfected the art of dying more than any other species on this earth, especially at lambing time, leaving the tedious task of fostering their lambs to other ewes, a task at which Alan excelled, with his endless patience and gentle perseverance. It also left the problem of collecting the carcasses, and as the ewes determinedly died as far from the lambing pens as they could decently manage, we soon discovered it was quicker and easier to use my mother's Morris Minor to collect them, loading the dead ewe into the boot and pulling her, without ceremony, onto the ground at the end of the lambing pens to await collection by the knackerman.

It was easier, too, collecting sick sheep with the Morris Minor, carefully loading the ewe into the boot and placing her lambs in the footwell behind the front seats. With Alan balancing on the rear bumper, holding onto the edge of the opened boot lid and the dreadful Cyril, almost lost from sight, twisting and turning, talking all the time, sitting in the passenger seat, we must have presented a strange spectacle as I slowly drove across the field to the pens.

Mr. Chubb witnessed it one day, and he was not amused.

'What would your mother say if she knew you were using her car for carting sheep around the field? What would her friends think if she drove them to a bridge party in a car smelling of dead sheep? I don't wish to tangle with your mother, I have enough problems running this farm as it is. You must not do it again.'

But of course we did.

'I reckons Mr. Chubb's bothered by your old lady,' said Alan with his toothless smile, 'an' it takes a lot to bother Mr. Chubb.'

ᖳ

4.
From Grand Tours to Silage Making

The solitary figure I had fleetingly glimpsed behind the doorway of the feed mill on my first morning at the farm had been Fred who ran the mill, mixing and grinding the rations for all the stock on the estate. He was also in charge of the dryer.

'I'm not sure it is a good decision to send you along with Fred when you have been here for such a short time,' Mr. Chubb told me. 'He can be a difficult man to understand and work with; you'll have to make of him what you will. There is little else for you to do on the farm at the moment and I thought it as good a time as any for you to meet Fred. He's a rogue, but I wouldn't be without him.' He hesitated. 'You'll find he has a rather odd sense of humour and a strong independent personality, but he is a marvellous worker.'

The feed mill was a building of massive construction with thick brick walls and heavy oak beams abutted into the brickwork. Thick planks of timber were laid on the closely spaced beams to form the floor of the first storey. A hatchway with two self-closing doors was set into the ceiling, above which there was a hoist. This was used to lift the two hundredweight bags of barley through the hatchway, the doors slamming shut as the heavy sacks cleared them, from where they were either tipped into the hopper which led down to the grinder, or were stored in topped heaps on the floor. The building needed to be strong with the deadweight of tons of corn stacked above.

The grinder and the hoist were powered by an impressively large electric motor, and when this was in motion a series of long rusty spindles, suspended from brackets bolted to the wall, rotated slowly: attached to these spindles were various pulleys and cast wheels, their original uses lost to memory, but retained because the hoist was operated from the very end of the run of the spindles. Various other disconnected drives led at right angles to the motor, seized solid from years of disuse, waiting to be dismantled and loaded onto a didicoy's lorry. Everywhere there was dust, a fine pervading white dust coating the floor, the walls and even the cobwebs, delicately weighting them down as if the mill was in the grip of a permanent hoar frost.

Above everything hung the unique smell of the feed mill, the residue of which lingered on my clothing long after I had left the place. It was a combination of the large population of farm cats, feral cats which had made the building their headquarters and ground barley – not dissimilar odours – spiced with linseed cake and dried sugar beet pulp. It was not too bad a smell when one became used to it, but for the fortnight I spent with Fred in the feed mill my mother insisted I bathed as soon as I came home.

The cats were Fred's. He was given a small allowance by the Major to feed them, though I suspected he topped them up with money from his own waistcoat pocket.

Mr. Chubb's comments had made me slightly apprehensive about my stay with Fred in his feed mill; I need not have worried. Fred and I shared a common interest in racing, and his interest was further aroused when he discovered my mother had an account with a local bookmaker. For some extraordinary reason she opened the account some years before solely to place bets on the Grand National and the Derby. My sister and I used it occasionally, but all that changed when I met Fred. He introduced me to 'cross doubles' and we used the account daily. I telephoned our bets through every lunchtime and, under Fred's tutelage, I prospered. My mother was not so happy.

'You really ought to try and save your money instead of throwing it away on the horses,' she said with a resigned sigh as she handed me the unopened account from the bookmaker one day, 'You will finish losing everything if you are not careful.'

Fred was too shrewd to allow that to happen: there were few weeks when the bookmaker required a cheque from us. I often wondered what he thought of my mother's sudden interest and expertise in the racing world after the account had been so little used over the years.

Fred belonged to the old school of Mr. Chubb's farmworkers, one of the many who had never made the transition from the horse to the tractor, remaining on the farm as manual labourers. He was a short, powerful man with broad shoulders, rather sunken bright blue eyes which flashed with devilment when an outrageous thought occurred to him, and no teeth. He was, I judged, in his late fifties, and he wore an old boiler suit rendered almost chalk white by the dust which frequent washing had failed to dislodge from the fibres, and a cap with his pipe, in moments of repose, firmly clipped behind the button of the peak. He prefaced nearly every sentence he spoke with the phrase, 'same as I says, you.'

The previous, and only farm student had been called David, and Fred had it immoveably fixed in his mind all students were called David and no amount of gentle persuasion could shake him from this belief. To him I was 'Davy' and remained so for all the time I knew him.

Fred was particularly proud of his lack of teeth.

'Same as I says, you,' he told me, 'I 'ad 'em all out when I were a nipper. When I walked into town to pick up me new 'uns, an' it were eight mile there an' eight mile back, mind, I got to the top of Stocks 'ill an' sat down for a breather. I took 'em out an' 'ad a good look at 'em. The buggers were already rubbing me gums an' making 'em sore. I 'eld 'em in my 'and an' thought what bloody silly looking things they was an' I thought if they 'ad caused me that pain in such a short time, what would they buggers do to me for the rest of my life. So I 'urled them down the 'illside as far as I could, an' I ain't 'ad none since.'

We spent the day mixing rations, unloading lorries, loading trailers, taking out the feed to the dairy and the various buildings housing the in-wintering cattle, mostly situated, for some reason, on the tops of inhospitable hills: the spring had been cold, with little growth to the grass and the cattle were still housed in their rickety draughty winter quarters.

Fred showed me how to operate the grinder. He picked up a heavy stick and brought it down hard on the tin cover. Clouds of choking white dust rose into the air.

'Same as I says, you, I always 'its that first to shift they cats. The buggers can get in there amongst they blades an' I forgot to 'it it once before I started 'er up an' two of my cats came flying out like minced meat, splattered all over the place they was. I ain't forgotten again.'

He led me over to the control box which was directly above the electric motor. It was a complicated affair, with a red and a green button – straightforward enough – and several small levers and reset buttons set into the frame on the sides and the top. A brass wheel protruded from the right-hand side of the box and a round glass-fronted ammeter from the top.

'First you presses the red button,' Fred instructed me, 'then you 'its this black 'un with your fist, then you lifts this little brass lever, presses the red 'un again an' slowly winds the wheel, at the same time pressing the green button with your left hand. If you winds the wheel too fast she blows 'er trip an' you 'as to start all over again, so watch the needle on the gauge, if she goes over half ways you'se winding too fast.'

James watched me innocently start the mill one morning, a look of astonishment on his face. 'What are you doing?' he asked.

I patiently explained I was starting the grinding mill.

'Look,' he said, pushing me to one side, 'all you have to do is press the green button and wind the handle. I suppose Fred taught you all this rigmarole?'

I nodded, and James wandered off in search of him, muttering something about the advisability of farm students learning anything from Fred.

Fred must have loved watching 'his student' as he called me, starting up the mill; it was almost a shame James had spoilt his fun, but I was coming to know Fred and his ways, his wayward sense of humour, his firm views from the way the farm should be run to politics and the declining standards of the young.

'Same as I says, you, they'se a bunch o' pansies; they doesn't know the meaning of work, all they wants is money for doing nothing.'

Having observed some of the youths of the village lounging around the buildings, smoking and throwing stones at Fred's cats after the school bus had returned them home, it was difficult to disagree. Some of them worked on the farm in the school holidays and they were, according to Fred, 'Worse than bloody useless.'

Fred's personality was as strong as his physique. In many ways he was like Mr. Chubb and they frequently argued and clashed; it was inevitable with two such forceful men, but they both held each other in grudging respect.

'Same as I says, you,' Fred said after a particularly heated argument with Mr. Chubb which Fred won with some ease, 'I's been with 'un for over thirty years an' 'ee wouldn't be without me.'

☘

The lateness of the spring meant the sheep still needed extra rations. Alan had taken a well earned holiday and it was left to Fred and I to feed them every afternoon. Mr. Chubb parked his Land Rover in the yard at about half past three, admonishing me to look after it and drive it with care as 'It is the best Land Rover the estate has ever given me, and I don't want it wrecked,' before walking home, his day done.

We hitched up the small Land Rover trailer, loaded it with hay and the concentrates and embarked on our 'grand tour'.

The sheep were on one of the far boundaries of the farm, about two miles away. We drove through the narrow twisting lanes, the banks thick and deep green with emerging cow parsley waiting for warmer weather before rushing into untidy tall blooms, transforming the banks into a sea of white, like deep drifts of snow; the hazel meeting high over the top of the lanes forming leafy tunnels in the summer, but now bare branches rubbing together in the wind, the leaf buds hardly breaking through. Carpets of fading primroses covered the floor of the coppices.

'Same as I says, Davy,' said Fred as if reading my thoughts, 'if only this bloody weather'd warm up an' the wind shift out of the north things'd soon start moving.'

The sheep were waiting for us. Fred untied the Hampshire gate, and I drove through. It was never easy feeding those greedy ewes. We tried distracting them by feeding the hay first, Fred standing unsteadily in the small trailer throwing it on the ground while I slowly drove along. The ewes picked at it, their lambs imitating them without quite knowing why, chewing stalks of hay, lifting their heads, watching their mothers and carelessly letting the sodden stalks drop, wasted, to the ground. The ewes were not fooled for a moment: it was the concentrates they were after.

As soon as Fred had thrown out the last wodge of hay, I sped to the troughs, followed by a mob of galloping, bellowing sheep. Leaping out of the Land Rover, I ran round to help Fred with the bags, but it was already too late: the ewes hemmed us in and we had to force our way to the troughs and try to fill them without too much wastage, dribbling feed from the bags over the ewes' heads, pouring the concentrates into clear spaces as quickly as we could while the ewes, no respecters of our legs, shoved and barged for room, burying their heads in the troughs, straining with their back legs almost horizontal, looking from the distance like a mass of woolly maggots. Some of the lambs were large enough to appreciate the taste of Fred's mixture; it was a wonder none were crushed to death.

We left the determined ewes licking out the troughs, some drifting slowly over to the hay to enjoy a more leisurely second course, closed the gate and embarked on our 'grand tour'.

CR

Many of the older farm workers, even in the 1960's, had never left the village in which they were born, although Fred was more widely travelled, having been to London once and adventurously taking his holidays across the water on the Isle Of Wight. He liked to keep ahead of his more prosaic colleagues, and our 'grand tours' were, in his mind, a means of accomplishing his aim.

'Turn left 'ere, Davy, we'll go down to Southwell Farm. I wants to see 'ow old Smithy got on with 'is drilling earlier.'

'Look at that,' said Fred when we arrived at the unfortunate farmer's field of corn. 'Bloody terrible. 'Ee ain't even rolled it proper. My cats would break their bloody legs if they walked over that.'

In the two weeks Alan was away, Fred and I inspected all the surrounding farms, parking Mr. Chubb's Land Rover in gateways, up tracks and, opening gates, we drove around the pastures criticising the stock. Fred, to his enormous satisfaction, found fault with everything, from the cattle and sheep to the crops and the state of the fences.

We hurtled up rough flint tracks, across fields and through farmyards, the trailer bumping and swaying dangerously at the rear, Fred sitting beside me in the front, bolt upright, waving regally to astonished farmworkers who gathered in our wake wondering what on earth was going on.

We covered miles in Mr. Chubb's Land Rover on these expeditions, and it was a wonder we were never stopped and questioned by Mr. Chubb's irate neighbours. We must have been observed, and everyone knew the Land Rover. Perhaps they thought it was Mr. Chubb himself recklessly roaring through their farmyards having taken temporary leave of his senses – it must have been difficult to see who was driving as we passed by in a blurred cloud of swirling dust – but we never heard a word, and Mr. Chubb never mentioned the extra miles we clocked up.

''Ee never looks at that dial anyways,' Fred said. 'An if 'ee does it's only to see how fast 'ee's going.'

I would not have worried if he had noticed the extra miles: Fred could talk his way out of any situation and, besides, he possessed the luck of the devil.

Our deadline for returning to the farm was half past four, for this was when the racing results were announced on the radio. We dumped the Land Rover in the yard and sat in my mother's Morris Minor, bent over the feeble radio straining to hear the presenter's voice, pencils poised.

One evening the door was opened and a puzzled James peered in.

'Whatever are you doing?' he enquired.

'Just mending Davy's radio,' Fred instantly replied.

James peevishly walked away. He was no match for Fred, and he knew it.

ଔ

Every Friday afternoon we took the week's rations down to the calf-rearing unit, which was run neatly, conscientiously and cleanly by Derek, a gentle bald man with enquiring eyebrows who always wore a spotless orange rubber apron over his clothing. There was no malice to Derek, but Fred couldn't abide him.

'A lazy bugger,' was his outrageous verdict on a man who had won countless prizes for the estate by the excellence of his stockmanship. Maybe it was Derek's very excellence that irritated Fred.

Our first visit to Derek's calf rearing unit was memorable. Fred jumped off the trailer to see me back. 'Keep coming, keep coming,' he called, waving his arm. 'Bit more, bit more.'

There was a bang and a tinkling of broken glass falling to the ground as the trailer hit the corner of the building.

'Whoa!' Fred yelled, then coming round to the tractor, 'That'll learn 'im.'

Quite what it would learn him was unclear. Derek came out and surveyed the wreckage. Shaking his head sadly he said to me, 'You wants to watch that Fred, 'ee'll lead you astray, nipper.'

The advice, I felt, had arrived too late.

ଔ

My working day started at 7.30, the same time as the farmworkers started. Even for a wage of £1 per week there were few concessions for the student, and rightly so for I was luckier than some of my fellow students working on farms in the area: their parents had to pay the farmer for the privilege of having their son working for him.

Living only three miles from the farm, I soon discovered the optimum time for setting the alarm clock. It was 6.40, and this time was decided for me by the eccentricities of the ancient, sometimes stubborn but always temperamental electric cooker my frugal mother had bought second-hand some years previously. She always had an eye for a bargain and had spotted the cooker languishing in a corner of her favourite junk shop for a knockdown price of two pounds. After she had paid the owner of the shop, she informed him she expected delivery and connection to the mains as part of the deal, and he grudgingly obliged: my mother was one of his best customers. The cooker became her pride and joy, but I hated the thing.

It had heavy solid cooking rings which either remained luke-warm for what seemed eternity or became red hot in no time at all. Cooking breakfast was a delicate juggling act. As soon as the alarm clock sounded with a clattering frenzy – I kept it in a tin wastepaper basket beside my bed for maximum effect – I rushed downstairs, turned the dreadful cooker on to full and placed the frying pan on one of the rings. After I had washed and shaved I returned to check its mood.

I was either greeted by clouds of astringent blue smoke floating gently up the stairs or a sulky, barely warm frying pan which refused to fry. These fits of temperament were probably caused by the highly dangerous wiring in the house for, even in the I960's, much of it was lead-sheathed cable.

My father, who usually came downstairs as I was eating half cooked or blackened bacon and fried bread, depending on the capriciousness of the cooker that morning, invariably flung open the outside door, observing irritably, 'You've burnt the fat again.'

One morning I overslept and only had time for baked beans on toast. 'You've burnt the fat again,' said my father as he opened the door.

The early ritual completed, I drove the short distance to the farm in my mother's Morris Minor. (On the rare occasions she needed her car I caught the 'bus and Mr. Chubb allowed me to arrive twenty minutes late.) I parked the car in the yard and was given my orders for the day.

When I arrived on the 'bus, Mr. Chubb left my instructions with Fred. One morning he came out of his feed mill to greet me.

'You'se with me today, Davy,' he said. 'We 'as a few jobs to do 'ere first, then we puts the trailer on your Fergie an' goes up to the silage clamp. We starts silaging Monday an' there's a tidy few jobs needs doing up there.'

While we were clearing the debris from the clamp Fred told me I was to drive one of the Fordsons during silage making, and I would be working with Brian and Wilf. Brian was the son of a farmworker from an adjacent farm, one of those Fred and I had inspected on our 'Grand tours' in Mr. Chubb's Land Rover. I had already met him: he was a pleasant young man of ready wit, about a year older than myself. Wilf, with whom I had barely exchanged a word, was about thirty-five, heavily bearded and running to seed at an early age. He had an impressive beer belly. He eschewed the boiler suits worn by his colleagues, preferring a more casual form of dress. He always wore a grubby tartan cap on his head.

'Same as I says, you, Wilf can be a funny bugger,' Fred told me. ''Ee ain't got no patience with nothing, and it don't take much to upset 'un.'

ᴄ&

We made a more concentrated attempt to tidy up the clamp later in the week, Wilf, Brian and Alan joining Fred and me.

The silage clamp was a deep depression bulldozed out of the chalk, some thirty yards long by ten yards wide, fashioned in such a way that a tractor and trailer could be driven through it, slowly tipping the trailer and spreading the grass more or less evenly at the same time. The forty-four gallon drums of molasses, buckets, shovels, prongs, chains, heaps of chalk and straw bales were ready. The silage sides were taken out of storage and fitted to the trailers, the slightly altered shapes of the trailers from the previous year necessitating the use of heavy hammers and bad language to achieve a good fit.

Fred was right, I had been promoted to a Fordson Power Major. It was a diabolical machine, lacking any refinement, not even boasting the basic canvas-clad Lambourne cab. Worst of all it 'hunted', surging forward on its own volition, dying a little before surging forward again. It was, apparently, the student's lot to drive the oldest, the most unreliable and, in some cases, the most dangerous tractors available. I was once given an elderly Nuffield. Quite apart from the fact its braking system was totally ineffective – standing on the brake pedal with all my weight merely produced a half-hearted grinding noise which did little to slow the machine – it also rained hot embers from its exhaust pipe onto my head, singeing my hair.

I envied Wilf his brand new Fordson Super Major which he was to use to power the forage harvester.

cs

An old Standard Fordson Major had been left by the side of the track leading to the silage clamp by some loggers who, during the winter, had used it to run their saw bench. As it protruded slightly onto the track we decided to tow it backwards some two hundred yards into a clearing, out of the way.

The taciturn Wilf, who was as unsure how to handle a farm student as I was unsure how to handle him, produced a long tow chain and we connected his tractor to the old Fordson.

'Get up there and steer,' he said imperiously, 'and I'll tow you up the clearing.'

With a jerk we got under way, and Wilf accelerated briskly up the track. The loggers had used the tractor as a stationary engine, and the winter rains had evidently penetrated the steering linkages. I could hardly move the steering wheel, and there was a steep drop to one side of the lane; there was no relief from the other side, which was a stout, thick hawthorn hedge. Standing up on the footplates, looking over my shoulder and using all my strength on the almost immovable wheel, I yelled at Wilf to stop. It was hopeless. He couldn't hear me and, staring resolutely forward, he increased his speed, unaware of my predicament at the end of his chain.

49

The standard Fordson started off in a series of small zig-zags, gradually increasing all the time as we approached the clearing, and despite my desperate corrections on the obstinate steering I was always about half a turn too late to keep a true course.

Wilf, blissfully unaware of his oscillating charge behind him, pulled up, jumped out of his tractor and bent to remove the drawpin securing the chain.

Thoroughly shaken, I told Wilf in no uncertain terms precisely what I thought of his driving.

'There ain't no need to take that tone, nipper,' he said huffily, 'you only 'ad to shout and I'd 'ave stopped.'

My arms ached for days afterwards.

ﾃ

My job was to drive alongside the forage harvester, in rotation with Brian, collecting the chopped and blown grass evenly in the trailer, no easy task with my inexperience and a machine which progressed in a series of fits and starts. I soon discovered if I positioned my tractor alongside Wilf's where I could read the 'Fordson Super Major' name badge on its bonnet from a certain angle, I was about right. Once the throttle was set to match the speed of the forage harvester the involuntary 'hunting' facility of my Fordson became almost an advantage, spreading the grass more or less evenly in the trailer with little effort and minimum wastage of the crop.

However, it was vital to keep 'Fordson Super Major' in its correct place, and I stared so hard at that name badge it became almost obsessive, the letters reversing themselves to 'nosdroF repuS rojaM' to relieve the tedium. To this day, when I see an old Fordson I think of it affectionately as a 'nosdroF'. It would have been difficult to have coped had the name badge fallen off the bonnet.

Once the trailer was loaded, I drove slowly back to the silage pit and tipped the sweet smelling chopped grass where it was attacked from all sides by a tractor and buckrake and men armed with 'four grained' prongs. The load was soon spread and Fred, relieved from his duties in the feed mill, wearing an apron that had once been orange but which was now encrusted with a covering of sticky black molasses, sloshed bucket loads of the stuff over the silage, himself and anyone who unwisely happened to be within his range. An elderly International crawler tractor completed the operation, driven back and forth over the molassed grass, compressing it until the next load arrived.

I enjoyed silage making. I liked the smell of the molasses mixed with the crushed fragrance of the grass, the cheerful banter in the silage pit and even the irritability of Wilf when I momentarily lost sight of 'nosdroF repuS rojaM' and grass was blown onto the ground behind the trailer. I enjoyed the afternoon tea break where the delicate sandwiches my mother prepared for me contrasted starkly with the enormous doorstep sandwiches the farmworkers' wives had prepared for their men. And they drank cold tea from lemonade bottles – a local taste, but one which I never acquired.

I enjoyed my tea break if it happened to be at the silage pit where Fred, playing to his audience, told me outlandish stories which, by their very exaggeration, must have started as a truth and, after years of incubation in his lively mind, emerged as distorted, entertaining versions of the originals. When the tea break occurred in the field, the noisy machinery was silenced, the roar of the harvester diminishing slowly as Wilf disengaged the power take off on his tractor, the blades falling neatly into their lines with a metallic, disorganised tapping like a blacksmith's hammer forging a horseshoe on an anvil. After the last blade had arranged itself there was peace: the sounds of nature re-established themselves in their own domain, the singing of the birds, the far off chopping of woodpeckers in the adjacent copse, disturbed only by Wilf noisily slurping his cold tea.

I enjoyed the overtime. I was allowed that over and above my £1 weekly wage. But most of all I enjoyed the relevance of silage making. Freed from the rigid constraints of school discipline, some of which seemed to me as useless as the algebra I had reluctantly assimilated, I felt I was doing something worthwhile for the first time in my life, and all this was achieved in the beauty of the countryside, in the company of uncomplicated men who understood both human nature and mother nature in the way a town dweller would find difficult to comprehend, and who lived in empathy with their countryside. There was little call for algebra here.

ભ

Wilf was having more trouble adjusting to a public school educated farm student than the student had adjusting to him, but gradually he unbent a little, accepting this unwanted intrusion into his settled way of life with grudging resignation. He had, after all, little option.

My expertise in driving alongside Wilf was improving and the heaps of blown grass which missed the high silage trailer were becoming less. I stopped on my way back to the silage pit to scatter the larger heaps of evidence of my inexperience with my boot in case Mr. Chubb should notice, carefully making sure Brian was collecting his load from Wilf and I was unobserved, but Fred missed nothing. Standing on the side of the silage pit, where the chalk had been thrown high by the bulldozer's blade, and which was covered in elder trees in full white saucer-shaped blooms, he called to me as I turned to enter the clamp.

'Same as I says, you, if you was to drive tighter to Wilf you wouldn't 'ave no need to clear up after, an' they cows would 'ave a tidy bit extra to eat in the winter.'

Despite Fred's admonition, I reckoned I had fully mastered silage making when I was brought to earth with a jolt by Wilf. He suddenly stopped his forage harvester and, unprepared, I continued down the field, grass spraying onto the ground behind. A hen pheasant, her head held low, ran flat out along the cut line, weaving before disappearing in the long grass, her progress marked by the swaying of the stems. Wilf had climbed out of his tractor, removed his tartan cap and was carefully transferring the eggs from her nest into it. I watched with interest.

'What are you going to do with them, Wilf?' I asked.

He looked up at me in astonishment, 'Eat them of course. What the bloody 'ell else can you do with pheasant eggs?'

Unhooking the army surplus haversack hanging from the cab of his tractor he removed his empty sandwich box and lined the bottom with handfuls of grass, gently placing the warm eggs into his man-made nest. A thought occurred to him.

''Ere, don't you go telling no one about this, nipper,' he said. 'It's like this, see. If I 'adn't seen 'er, she'd 'ave gone up the spout of that 'arvester an' landed in the trailer in a cloud of feathers like Fred's cats gets ground up in 'is mill, all guts an' fur, so I ain't done no 'arm, but them keepers sees it different. Look,' he went on, trying to buy my silence, 'you 'ave some, nipper – they eats lovely 'ard boiled.'

The thought of eating hard-boiled, part-hatched pheasant eggs frankly appalled me, and I declined Wilf's offer.

'They pheasants is stupid,' he said, endeavouring to justify himself, 'mostly they just sits tight an' the 'arvester sucks 'em up, eggs an' all. That 'un were lucky I see 'er. You won't say nothing, nipper?' he said anxiously. 'There's others 'ere what don't understand.'

He grinned suddenly, his hairy face becoming animated and friendly. 'I often wonders what they cows thinks when they chews their silage in winter an' comes across a bundle of feathers, bones and smashed egg shells.'

Chuckling at his own joke, he climbed onto his tractor and we resumed silaging, Wilf scanning the ground ahead for sitting pheasants.

⋈

The weather was not always kind during my first silaging, and on wet days Mr. Chubb assigned us a miscellany of jobs. The most unpopular of these was clearing the dung from the long farrowing sheds which had once housed the pigs on which the farm's fortunes had been based. They had been roughly converted into cattle sheds where the young stock from Derek's calf-rearing unit spent the winter, living in concrete cubicles which accommodated three or four calves. The central alleyway, which had pens on either side, was too narrow to allow a tractor and trailer entry, and the only way of removing the dung was by forking it over the walls of the cubicles into wheelbarrows and tipping it into a heap outside. There were about thirty cubicles in all, piled so high with a mixture of dung and straw that the calves, at the back end of the winter, sometimes jumped down into the alleyway. Clearing these cubicles was a daunting task, and on one dismal drizzly day Mr. Chubb sent Wilf, Brian and myself to attack the tightly compressed dung with our four-grained prongs. Prising it from the corners and gullies strained the muscles, causing Wilf, who was the least physically fit of us, to grunt and grumble, the sweat pouring from his brow, dripping into his eyes and aggravating his considerable temper.

It was hardly surprising that, after an hour or so of desultory dung clearing, boredom took over. At the entrance to the old farrowing shed was a large ante room which had once contained boilers for cooking the pig swill. It was used as a storeroom when the calves were in residence; Fred and I had made many journeys there in the winter, stocking it with calf food and bales of straw and hay, but now it was empty, the rough concrete floor bare.

During our tea break, Brian found an old baked bean tin on one of the windowsills. It had probably been used to store syringes. He threw it to the floor where it clanged on the concrete and rolled to a halt, the echoes ringing round the empty ante room with exaggerated volume.

'Let's 'ave a game of football,' said Brian, kicking the tin to Wilf.

'Do what?' Wilf asked. 'Mr. Chubb'd sack us if 'ee were to find us playing football when we's supposed to be shifting this shit.'

'There ain't no danger of that,' said Brian, 'I see 'im an' James going out in 'is car, an' they was all dressed up smart. They won't be back till after dinner.'

Soon the three of us were playing a fast, furious noisy game of football, chasing the tin around the room. It was a change from the back-breaking work of dung clearing.

The game ended abruptly and disastrously as is so often the way on such occasions. Wilf aimed a mighty kick at the tin, missed and stubbed his toe on a ledge in the concrete with the full force of the swing of his leg. He hopped around in agony, swearing violently before subsiding to the floor. We unlaced his boot and watched with interest as his big toe appeared to swell visibly, turning a startling shade of purple at the same time.

'You done it now, Wilf,' Brian told him. 'When Mr. Chubb finds out what happened 'ee'll sack you for sure.'

'Don't make I wild, Bri,' said Wilf through clenched teeth, the thought of the sack suddenly overcoming the pain from his toe, 'what the bloody 'ell do we tell 'im?'

We concocted a weak and hasty story that a full wheelbarrow of dung had tipped over and caught Wilf on the toe. It was the best we could think of in a short time. Brian and I loaded Wilf onto the trailer and drove him back to the farm. He was rushed to hospital: the big toe was broken and he was off work for a month.

cs

Mr. Chubb was, not unnaturally, furious. He knew perfectly well how his farm workers entertained themselves when they were supposed to be carrying out boring jobs on wet days and he strongly smelt a rat. He would have none of our story, and cross-examined Brian and I – and, later, Wilf – countless times, but we stuck to our line, and the more he questioned us the more obstinate we became. Perhaps we even came to believe a barrow really did fall on Wilf's toe, but Mr. Chubb certainly did not. At our weekly lunches he primed me with drinks in the hope of discovering the truth, to no avail.

Wilf was worried almost out of his mind I might crack under Mr. Chubb's interrogation, and I kept him on tenterhooks, relaying him distorted accounts of Mr. Chubb's questioning and hinting that I might be weakening: it did him no harm.

Eventually the matter died down and a relieved Wilf returned to work, but Mr. Chubb never quite forgot the incident of Wilf's toe. Years later he said to me 'You remember that cock and bull story you told me about a barrow falling on Wilf's toe? You can tell me now what really happened.'

Mindful that Wilf was still very much employed by Mr. Chubb, I replied, 'the barrow really did fall on his toe.' He sniffed dismissively. 'That damned public school code of yours; I suppose it is ingrained for life.' He leant forward, his finger pointing at me. 'I will find out the truth one day.'

Maybe he will.

ෆ

Silaging was almost completed. Brian was promoted to the forage harvester and the dour Harry took his place driving the silage cart. The silage pit became satisfyingly full, the winter feed for the dairy herd assured.

It was the very fullness of the pit that almost caused another disaster. It became impossible to drive through it without sinking deep into the soft molassed grass which rose to a hump in the middle. Alan backed to the entrance, connected a tow chain to the front axle of the Fordsons and slowly pulled us through in turn with the crawler tractor. On one of the last days of silaging, he towed me through the pit as I pulled the hydraulic lever which raised the trailer. Halfway up the 'hump' I glanced behind. The trailer was fully extended, the three shining hydraulic rams slowly dripping oil, the dirty underside of the trailer towering as high as a double-decker bus. The grass must have become jammed, for I could tell by the tyres the load was still there, and I could hear the corrugated iron tailboard banging as we lurched through the uneven pit. I looked forward at Alan, anxiously watching his charge. Suddenly his face registered alarm.

'Jump,' he shouted, 'She's going over.' A quick look behind confirmed his advice, one wheel was several feet off the ground – the unstable trailer must have ridden over a lump of grass – and I hurled myself off the tractor, landing and rolling in the silage, covering my clothing in the syrupy molasses and sticky grass. The rear wheel of the Fordson rose into the air: there was a loud crack as the drawbar snapped, the wheel returned to the ground and the trailer went over on its side, the body wrenched from the chassis.

Fred handed me his prong. 'Same as I says, you, seein' you 'ad 'er over, you'd best get in there an' shift all that grass out before we gets 'er back on 'er wheels.'

For a moment I almost believed him.

ෆ

55

We covered the pit down with chalk and straw. The whole operation had gone almost without a hitch, but it was the last year the old silage clamp, surrounded by oak trees and with the elder bushes growing on its banks, was used. Modernisation was in the air.

Mr. Chubb had only paid brief visits to see how the silaging was progressing. We all knew what we were doing, even a student under instruction, and he knew it too; if it worked, leave it alone was his philosophy, and it worked.

CB

5.
Haymaking, Ringworm and Warbles

Wilf's toe had mended by the start of haymaking, although he affected a limp and the occasional wince of pain. I had started a summer cold which, aggravated by the dust, refused to go away.

Haymaking began with a false flourish of wonderfully warm June weather which was soon replaced by a humid, thundery hot spell, bringing operations to an indefinite halt, leaving sodden swaths of hay lying untouched and deteriorating in the fields. Tempers became ragged, even the normally placid Mr. Chubb becoming irritable.

'Same as I says, you,' Fred told me, 'it 'appens every year. We 'as a drop of rain an' 'ee thinks 'aying's ruined, but I tells you one thing: the weather always comes right in the end, an' so do 'ee. I remembers one year,' he continued, contradicting himself, 'when it never did stop raining during 'aying, an we 'ad to push it all up in an 'eap an' burn it. We 'ad the finest crop of mushelrooms you ever saw in that patch in the autumn, an' they was delicious. We ate them for weeks, but this weather won't last, you'll see.'

∞

Mr. Chubb sent Brian, Wilf, Alan and I 'dung cart' whilst we waited for the weather to temper, clearing some cattle yards which were situated on top of a bleak hill. Why they were built in such a Godforsaken place was a mystery. In winter the wind howled through the buildings with a ferocity that threatened to lift the roof and blow out the windows, and the driving rain had long since stripped the buildings of their last vestiges of paint. Perversely, Mr. Chubb's cattle thrived on top of their lonely Hampshire hill in spartan conditions, rewarding him with ornate silver cups from the summer shows which he proudly displayed on the sideboard in his dining room. I often wondered whether it was these winter-quarters, with their rattling doors and windows, which accounted for the undeniably wild nature of the cattle, or whether it was something to do with their breeding.

There were no such doubts with Wilf. His was all in the breeding. I had never witnessed him really losing his temper, merely bouts of irascibility, but, from what I had gleaned, from time to time Wilf lost all control of himself. The farmworkers were curiously reticent when I pressed them for details. 'You'll see soon enough, nipper,' was the standard reply to my enquiries. Soon enough proved to be clearing dung from the cattle yards.

The interruption to haymaking was unwelcome; it spoiled the flow of the job and stop-gap work such as dung cart was always undertaken in a half-hearted manner, unlike when it was the main work of the week. Then we worked together with enthusiasm.

Wilf had fitted the dung fork to the front of his tractor and a heavy concrete weight to the rear. Mr. Chubb had recently purchased several Fordson 'Dexta' tractors to replace the reliable Ferguson 35's – although he still retained 'my' 35 and Brian, Alan and I were using them to cart the dung. These Dextas looked wrong, heavy and low on the front and light and high on the back: they were good road tractors with a remarkable turn of speed, but no match to the reliable Ferguson in the field.

'Wouldn't pull the skin off a rice pudding,' was Wilf's scathing verdict after he had tried one out. Wilf was loading my trailer when he struck an obstinate lump of shiny hardened dung. The dung fork constantly rode over it, and after several attempts to shift it had failed the engine note of the tractor rose in direct proportion to Wilf's temper. Brian had joined me, and we stood together watching Wilf's vain attempts to spear the dung. Brian's eyes were bright with anticipation as the enraged Wilf took longer and longer charges at the intractable heap, engine roaring, black smoke forced high into the air from the upright exhaust pipe. The yard had an imperceptible downward slope and inevitably he overreached himself, the front wheels of the tractor following the dung fork over the foot high hardened mass. He was unable to extricate himself driving forwards- the wall of the yard was only two feet from the front of his Fordson – and reversing, despite the heavy concrete weight attached to the three-point linkages, was equally impossible, Great clods of dung flew from the wildly spinning rear wheels, the front wheels lifting an inch or two up the object of Wilf's fury before returning gently to the concrete.

Wilf jumped off the tractor, turned through 180 degrees and, forgetting his recently mended big toe, kicked the tyre as hard as he could. The pain must have been considerable, for he hopped around the yard uttering expletives which would have pleased Fred. Brian and I watched, silently, entranced. While the pain was wearing he raged about his tractor, dung cart, Mr. Chubb and anything that happened to occur to him. Suddenly calm, he climbed back onto his tractor and tried again, easing it as close to the wall as he dared, giving it full throttle in a futile attempt to lift the front wheels backwards over the dung. The result was the same: steam rose from the overheated tyres in empathy with Wilf's overheated temper. Once more he leaped out of the tractor, pausing for a second with his arms held out like a fledgling about to take its first flight, his body bent at a forty-five degree angle to the ground. He straightened and, grasping his tartan cap by the peak, hurled it onto the filthy concrete with all his strength and vigorously jumped up and down on it for a few seconds. It was a remarkable performance. Picking up his cap, he unthinkingly replaced it on his head. This seemed to settle him. We heard the engine of Alan's tractor, returning for his next load. Wilf became panic-stricken and fretful.

'Bloody 'ell,' he said, 'that's all three of youse empty an' me stuck down there an' I cain't do nothing about it. What 'appens if Mr. Chubb comes up an' sees this mess? I don't know what 'ee'll say.'

' 'Ee'll probably sack you,' said Alan cynically. 'After the trouble with your toe it won't take much for 'ee to sack you.'

' 'Ee might be golfing today,' Wilf said hopefully, 'an' 'ee mightn't come up 'ere.'

' 'Ee ain't golfing,' Alan replied. 'I just seen 'un.'

Wilf pulled open his shirt and distractedly scratched his hairy chest with thick dung-encrusted fingers.

'We'd best use Bri to tow you out,' Alan observed, 'or, failing that, we'll 'ave to dig you out.'

Wilf unlooped the heavy tow chain from the spiked radiator guard of his Fordson. Brian reversed his Dexta to the stranded tractor and, revving his engine as hard as Wilf had tried his temper, failed to move him. Wilf had been correct in his judgement of the Dexta: it really could not pull the skin off a rice pudding. He shrugged his shoulders helplessly, standing dejectedly in the yard, rolling a dung-flavoured cigarette.

'We'll 'ave to dig 'im out,' said Alan.

Attacking the dung with our four-grained prongs soon revealed the cause of Wilf's predicament: the dung was concealing the concrete base of a long forgotten water trough.

'You'll 'ave to fetch the crawler up from the farm, Brian told him, 'an' if Mr. Chubb sees you 'ee'll 'ave you this time.'

'You do make I wild, Bri,' Wilf flared, 'It weren't my fault I got stuck.'

'That ain't the way 'ee'll see it,' Brian replied, ''Ee knows your tantrums.'

Wilf walked his lonely way down the hill, returning half-an-hour later with the crawler tractor. Mr. Chubb never put in an appearance. There was little dung carting done that afternoon.

୦ଓ

59

As the weather improved, the glass started rising and the clouds dispersed. The sun shone warmly on the dampened fields of mown grass and my summer cold became worse, mocking the healthy illusion of farm life.

I had noticed how the farmworkers were affected by the various moods of Mr. Chubb: when work progressed smoothly without hindrance from rain or breakdown, they reflected his cheerfulness and humour. The converse was true in times of crisis – there were many of these I was discovering – or interruption from perverse weather.

A fellow student worked on a neighbouring farm where the manager was as dour and glum as Harry. There was, he told me, no sense of fun or humour on that farm, the work undertaken as a necessary chore to earn money to feed the family, with little interest and continual bickering. I was thankful my father had placed me with Mr. Chubb.

Haymaking restarted at full pace. It was always a time fraught with uncertainty, a race against the weather that could never compare with the harvesting of any other crop, for a protracted wet spell could ruin days of work and expense in an astonishingly short time.

There were fields scattered across the farm in various states of readiness, from the newly mown to those almost ready to bale. I alternated between an ancient tedder, a machine which fluffed out the hay for the sun and wind to cure, and an equally ancient hay turner; the student was not to be trusted with the more sophisticated equipment.

Mr. Chubb drove his Land Rover across the field while I was tedding, heedless of the hay crushed beneath the wheels. I felt miserable with my cold, and he looked at me closely.

'You know the best cure for that cold of yours?' he asked.

Remembering my father's advice – bed and a bottle of whisky – I repeated it hopefully to Mr. Chubb. He chuckled to himself, slowly shaking his head.

'That's not right at all,' he said. 'What you need is a good woman, that will soon cure your cold.'

I stared as he drove out of the field, my cold forgotten.

ભ

Wilf was a man for most seasons, perhaps on account of his relative youth. In winter he was in charge of the sugar beet harvester, he drove a combine during the harvest, and, mostly, the forage harvester at silage making. For a man with such a terrific temper it was a wonder any of these temperamental machines survived his onslaughts when they broke down – which they did with a monotonous regularity – and it is a tribute to British engineering they survived Wilf. Inevitably, he was the man who baled the hay.

We worked long hours making that hay, and even longer hours carting it and stacking it in the barns, some of which were as diversely scattered around the farm as the apparently random locations of the hayfields: it was, Mr. Chubb told me, all part of the rotation. I really enjoyed those halcyon days of haymaking. My cold had moderated sufficiently for me to appreciate the almost indescribable sweet smell of the mixtures of drying grasses; the scents released as the vintage tedder clattered through the crop were scents of which I could never tire, like the bouquet of a perfect wine, and there was always the thought of making the hay for feeding to the sheep and cattle in the grim winter months. The same thought was reciprocated on cold January days, standing half-frozen on the back of a trailer, wearing layers of sweaters and two pairs of socks, flakes of snow falling from a darkening sky, cutting open those bales of well made hay and throwing thick wodges of it to the sheep, the fragrance recalling those fine June days, sending a reminder that another summer was not impossibly faraway.

'Take a little sunshine into the barn,' was a well used phrase, and we stacked plenty of sunshine in the farm's barns that year. On grey, dismal days when the hay was fed, that trapped sunshine briefly came out and illuminated the winter scene.

Towards the end of haymaking, and while the weather held, every last paddock was cut. I was tedding a tiny two-acre piece when Mr. Chubb arrived in the adjacent paddock, incongruously towing 'my' hay turner behind his Land Rover. He opened the gate and started driving round the windrows. Nothing happened, for he had neglected to change the wheels from the 'transport' position to the 'operating' position which swung the turner out into the hay. After several ineffectual passes he came over to me.

'How does this bloody thing work?' he asked. I showed him. New-fangled ideas,' he muttered.

It was one of the oldest items of machinery on the farm.

◌౩

In the early 1960's the most modern form of bale stacking in the field was achieved by a wooden sledge, mounted on steel runners and towed behind the baler. As each bale was made, it was stacked on the sledge and when the stack was completed, a long heavy bar was lifted, tipping the wooden floor of the sledge, allowing the stack to slide gracefully to the ground. There was a knack to using this thing, and often the bales collapsed into an untidy heap, the stacker earning a stream of derision from Wilf, comfortably seated in his tractor. It was hard, dusty work, trying to balance on the lurching sledge, at the same time endeavouring to build a neat stack.

At last the baling was completed, the fields shaved bare of their tall grasses, looking as though they would never grow again from the sun hardened earth. In every field bales awaited transport to the barn, and then the real work started – there was little easy tractor driving here.

The student was never given the light work, and at first Mr. Chubb allocated me to loading the trailers in the field. A petrol-engined elevator, with a long canvas belt driving a large cast-iron wheel, was hitched to the rear of the trailer, and it was my job to throw the bales onto the elevator. The canvas belt was a constant source of irritation, frequently detaching itself from the wheel, hurling itself onto the ground where it lay like a gigantic coiled snake. The engine, never the easiest to start, was silenced, the belt retrieved and replaced, and the heavy crank vigorously wound until reluctant puffs of white smoke issued from the circular exhaust pipe and the engine fired, settling down to a steady thumping rhythm.

As each stack was cleared, I pulled a lever on the side of the elevator which operated a dog clutch, stopping the wooden slats from rotating, and moved the tractor on. The driver remained on the trailer. The first tractor into the field after lunch one day was Wilf's,

'If you loads me up fast, nipper,' he said craftily, 'you can 'ave a rest afore the next tractor comes.'

I took him at his word, throwing bales onto the elevator as fast as I could, and they rained around him. Wilf, softened by too much tractor driving and too much beer, was perspiring liberally, hardly knowing which bale to pick up first. He barely had time to clear the backlog before we arrived at the next stack. He left the field exhausted for whatever purpose he had in mind.

Wilf was right. I had plenty of time before the arrival of the next tractor. Looking for something to do, I decided to grease the dog clutch on the elevator. Alan was next on the rotation and his entrance into the field coincided with that of James.

James had called in on his way to a farm walk and he was immaculately dressed in cavalry twill trousers, a smart mustard waistcoat and his best cap which shamed the dreadful tartan cap worn by Wilf. His brown brogues were polished to the standard of his national service days and his tweed jacket completed the illusion of a gentleman farmer out for the day.

Hitching the elevator onto the back of Alan's trailer I started the engine. James, standing by the elevator, waited until Alan was ready and let in the dog clutch. There was a soft spluttering sound. Holding the first bale ready, the twine biting into my fingers, I looked at James in disbelief. I had evidently overgreased the clutch and when he had engaged it globules of black grease had liberally splattered him from his brogues to his cavalry twills, up his mustard waistcoat and even onto his best cap. He wiped the back of his hand across his face, spreading the grease from cheek to cheek: he looked like a parody of a circus clown.

It was difficult not to laugh. James wisely left the field in silence. Wilf, I thought, had a lot to answer for.

⋈

I found haymaking tiring work, not in the least helped by my cold. When I returned home, I ate a hasty meal and quickly retired to bed. This worried my mother.

'It's not normal for someone of your age to be so tired,' she said, 'there must be something wrong with you. I will make an appointment with the doctor – perhaps you need a tonic.'

Wearily I explained there was nothing wrong with me and the last thing I needed was a visit to the doctor's surgery. It was merely a combination of hard physical work, which I was unused to, dust, the heat and, most of all my cold for which, I assured her, no doctor had yet discovered a cure.

The following day Mr. Chubb told me he was changing me over with Wilf. I was to drive his tractor, carting the bales, and he was to load the elevator.

'It's about time Wilf did some manual work,' Mr. Chubb said, 'he's becoming much too fat, and you need more experience in tractor driving.'

Wilf was furious and I was deeply suspicious. 'It ain't right the bloody student should 'ave the easy work,' he said to me, 'an' I 'as to give 'im my tractor an' do all the 'umping. You ain't been 'ere for five minutes an' youse treated like you ain't one of us, an' I tells you, that ain't bloody right.'

I agreed, privately, with Wilf: it wasn't bloody right.

Mr. Chubb, beaming, stopped me in the lane just before lunchtime.

'It's much better you are tractor driving now,' he said, 'it will help your cold too.'

By this time I felt uncomfortable driving Wilf's tractor, suffering his pained looks as he threw the bales onto the elevator, staring hard and breathing heavily as he steadily stalked back to move his tractor on. I asked Mr. Chubb if, by any chance, my mother had had a hand in this. He, in his turn, looked uncomfortable.

'She did telephone me last night,' he admitted, 'and said you seemed a little tired, and I suggested a spell of tractor driving might help.'

I knew perfectly well this was nonsense. I knew my mother better than Mr. Chubb did, and I felt I knew Mr. Chubb well enough to tell him my thoughts.

'My cold is much better today,' I told him truthfully, 'and it makes me look foolish having special treatment just because my mother worries about her son's common cold. I am perfectly fit to throw those bales on the elevator. Besides,' I added dangerously, 'I overheard Wilf asking Alan, 'Who runs this bloody estate – 'im or Davy's mother?'

Mr. Chubb looked at me thoughtfully, running his hand around his chin.

'I will tell you what I will do,' he said. 'It's true you seem much better, and I agree you are probably right in what you say, so I'll put Wilf back on tractor driving and you can continue loading. I have kept part of my bargain with your mother – and I have no desire to fall foul of her – but,' he added darkly, pointing his index finger at my chest, 'if I hear another word from your mother I will send Wilf back to loading.' He turned and walked back to his Land Rover, his head bent.

Wilf was jubilant. 'That'll learn you, nipper,' he said with a hairy grin. 'Your old lady cain't always 'ave 'er own way, and you cain't 'ide be'ind 'er frock in the real world. Now move over to that 'eap an' get loading me.'

Fred, who knew everything that happened on the estate, was impressed. 'Same as I says you,' he told me, slowly shaking his head in awe, 'it takes a lot to frighten Mr. Chubb. 'Ee won a medal in the war, but I reckon your old lady's too much for 'im to 'andle. An' I reckons another thing, 'ee never 'ad 'er in mind when 'ee told you you needed a good woman to cure your cold.'

∞

Mr. Chubb had been walking the ground with a worried air, glancing from the sky to the stacks of bales in the hay fields awaiting transport to the barn.

'I don't trust those weather forecasters on the wireless,' I overheard him tell Fred, 'I think we will make an all out effort over the next few days to fetch in all the bales before the weather breaks.'

'You knows best, Mr. Chubb,' Fred replied, 'but they forecasts it fine all week an' I doesn't see no need to 'urry. Besides, a drop o' rain won't 'urt they bales, specially since they's stacked.'

'I know all that, Fred,' Mr. Chubb replied irritably, ' but I want all these bales cleared and in the barn. You can lend a hand in the field and I'll send Harry up with an extra tractor and trailer. We'll have them in under shelter in no time at all, you'll see.'

'You'se probably right,' said Fred, 'though I still doesn't see no need for 'aste.'

While Mr. Chubb prowled the fields in his Land Rover like a predatory fox, glancing left and right, meandering around the open ground in the same manner as he drove along the narrow lanes, one hand loosely holding the steering wheel, Fred and I loaded the bales at a terrific rate, sending the tractors and trailers out of the field in record time.

'Same as I says you,' Fred grumbled, 'I doesn't know why 'ee's in such a mad-rush to get they bloody bales in, but it's the same every year. 'Ee's always been the same, wanting to clear the job up an' start on the next 'un an' that James, 'ee ain't no better. Ee'll 'ave 'imself an 'eart attack one day if 'ee don't slow down, all rush an' tear 'ee is.

James often helped with the loading, stacking bales on the trailer. Once, when he was helping Alan, kneeing the bales high up onto the load, fitting each one into place like parts of a jigsaw puzzle, the belt flew off the elevator and I went to shut down the engine.

'There ain't no need for that, Davy,' said Fred, picking up his stick which for some reason he always carried with him in the hayfield – 'we'll soon 'ave the bugger back on again without all that fuss.'

With his stick held under his arm he refitted the belt around the larger wheel of the elevator, and running the stick along the inside of the belt brought it back to the fast rotating pulley at the engine end. Using the stick as a lever he slowly eased the belt onto the pulley; smoke rose as the edge of the pulley wheel wore into the hard hazel.

James, suddenly aware of Fred's dangerous manoeuvre, jumped off the trailer, ran to the engine and pushed over the sprung piece of metal which shorted the sparking plug. As the engine slowly died the belt finally slid onto the pulley and Fred triumphantly tucked his smoking stick back under his arm.

'Don't you ever do that again,' James said. 'You could kill yourself. It was stupid to try.' He glanced from Fred to me. 'And it's no way for a student to learn,' he continued, 'following an example like that. I thought you would have known better, Fred.'

Fred was unrepentant. 'Same as I says, you,' he replied, 'I's been putting belts back on they bloody elevators for years like that an' I ain't never come to no 'arm. Now we's got to fire that bloody engine up again.'

He threw his stick down on the ground and, leaning forward, said to James, 'The trouble with you bloody nippers these days is you thinks you knows everything, an' just because that fancy college you went to says you 'as to do things proper don't always mean it's the best way. Come on, Davy, swing that bloody engine into life an' lets get on an' waste no more time.'

The enigmatic Harry, whom Mr. Chubb had added to the bale carting rota, was a man of few words to most and none at all to me. He affected a bale hook, a curved pointed piece of hardened metal with a wooden handle and he thrust this gruesome looking instrument into the bales as though he were handling endless carcasses at an abattoir rather than the more wholesome hay. He cut a sinister figure, silently stacking, the sweat pouring from his brow, misting his cheap circular framed spectacles and gluing his greasy felt hat to his head. He was incredibly ugly, his wide furrowed nose and sallow pockmarked skin giving him the appearance of a villain in a low budget film.

Wilf had returned from lunch with his empty trailer while Fred and I were loading Harry, and he helped pass the bales which were dropping off the end of the elevator almost faster than Harry could manage. He was slightly slow in turning for one, and it fell on his left shoulder, catching him a glancing blow. The result was astonishing. Harry threw the bale hook down, dropped to the bed of the trailer and writhed in apparent agony. I was amazed, for the bales were far from heavy.

Fred and Wilf were not impressed, standing back without speaking, watching while Harry appeared to be in his death throes.

Wilf sensed my enquiry. 'Don't take no notice, nipper,' he said, 'it's the way 'ee is. 'Ee ain't 'urt an' 'ee'll be 'imself presently.'

After a few seconds Harry stood up, dusted himself down, checked his glasses and hat were still in place, retrieved his bale hook and stood by the end of the elevator awaiting the next bale.

It had been a curious performance, and Harry had not uttered a single word throughout.

 C8

For the last two days of bale cart Mr. Chubb moved me into the barn. He was pleased with himself.

'Fred can cope with loading,' he said to me, 'and you can see the other end of the job in the barn while we finish off. Those weather forecasters were wrong,' he went on, beaming. 'I always knew they were. They now forecast rain in a day or two's time, but I knew that all along. There is no substitute for experience.'

Compared with the fresh air in the field, the barn was stiflingly claustrophobic and humid with sweating hay. An elevator, the same as the one we used in the field, lifted the bales so far: thereafter it was all manual, the bales passed from one person to the next, higher and higher until the roof was reached. It was no joke working under that corrugated iron roof, the heat from the unseen sun and the heat of the hay combining to make stacking an energy sapping chore, and all the time there were the fumes from the petrol engine of the elevator, far below, poisonously drifting up.

There was a wonderful sense of relief when the last bale from the trailer was on the elevator, jerking its way up the wooden slats, for even if there were some six left in the chain leading to the roof there was the prospect of a momentary sit-down while the next trailer was reversed to the elevator. It was a bonus if there had been a delay in the field and we had a real break before we heard the familiar strident engine beat of the next tractor. Then we wearily and stiffly roused ourselves from our comfortable positions on the soft bales and restarted the demanding elevator. There was little backchat in that stifling barn: the work was far too onerous.

Nothing is more satisfying when haymaking than to nudge the last bale of the season in place and then enjoy a good thunderstorm, listening the amplified noise of the rain beating down on the tin roof and watching the water pour from the downpipes, soaking the waste hay on the ground outside. That is exactly what happened at the end of my first haymaking.

The weather broke with a vengeance and it rained for days, but it no longer mattered. As Mr. Chubb remarked with feeling at our weekly lunch, 'That's haying done for another year.'

෪

After several months working as a farm student for Mr. Chubb my parents, I sensed, were having serious doubts concerning the way the experience was affecting their son. Private education was deemed a privilege, but it was also a sheltered existence, and those who left their public schools to enter what were, in the 1960's, called the professions, smoothly progressed from one institution to another: it was really very little different from school at all, and like a large club everyone knew each other by personal friendship or by reputation. It was, and probably still is, the old boy network.

There was no old boy network operating for the farm student; he was on his own, throwing off years of cloistered boarding school life to find out how the world operated, and this was a real worry for my parents. It was not so for me, for I was enjoying myself and my new found freedom, but it was difficult when spending a day with Fred, who prefaced nearly every noun he spoke with an adjectival expletive, not to pick up the repetitious habit. It was no help one time after a morning spent in his company to ask my mother what was for lunch in Fred's catching idiom.

I was washing my hands at the time and she pretended not to hear, but shortly afterwards I was taken to one side by my father and informed it was not the done thing for the sons of naval officers to be seen drinking beer in the public bars of public houses. I was, he told me, becoming like a farm hand. He was quite right. I was, as he put it, becoming like a farm hand but the structure of the Royal Navy and public school had never allowed for situations such as this, and adjustments had to be made on both sides to maintain harmony. And they were made, for I was not the only one learning.

෪

The farm student was a novelty, scarcely taken seriously, the butt of jokes and was tested hard to find his mettle. After I settled in I found I could give as good as I got. One day, after lunch, I pressed the starter on my Fordson only to find someone had plugged the drainhole of the upright exhaust pipe and poured a bucket of water down it. I was saturated, for there was no cab on the tractor. I strongly suspected Len who, from the early days of potato riddling had been on and off the farm in his capacity as a casual worker more times than I could remember. He was cunning, knowing Mr. Chubb was not enamoured with him, leaving hours in advance of the sack to take his next casual job in the area and returning when the farm needed him in moments of flat out work such as haymaking. He was a renowned practical joker, and I resolved to take my revenge on him. In the event, this proved unnecessary for Len, at least temporarily, cured himself of practical joking. He had developed the habit of hiding himself, and as I went by on my tractor shouting 'Whoa' in his stentorian tones, black skid marks on the road bearing testimony to my reactions.

I was backing my tractor and trailer in the yard one afternoon when I heard Len's reverberating 'Whoa', which I ignored as I had become thoroughly used to it. To my surprise, there was a screech of brakes and I looked round to see a red-faced Mr. Chubb peering out of the sliding side window of his Land Rover at an even redder-faced Len, who had emerged from behind the wall where he had been hiding, to see my reaction. No words were exchanged: they stared at each other for a while in silence, and Mr. Chubb drove away leaving a chastened Len to reflect upon the startlingly unexpected outcome of his joke.

There was never any malice attached to this humour; it was all a part of the farming life. I learnt to tell when I was being teased – Fred was by far the worst offender – or when there were more serious overtones, and when Fred informed me we were ringworming the following week I knew he was speaking in earnest.

'Same as I says, you, I 'ates that bloody job,' he said. 'Worst job on the farm. We warble flies at the same time, an' when they things explodes in your face it ain't no joke. An' itch. As soon as you sees they cattle up in an 'eap milling around the yard, all covered in them scabs, you'll start itchin' an' scratchin' all over, an' you'll itch an' scratch all day an' all night long.'

I watched Fred closely for signs of deliberate misinformation but, for once, he was deadly serious; he really did hate 'warbling an' ringworming.'

∞

Mondays, for some deeply buried reason were, and still are, always the days for shifting cattle from one pasture to another, or yarding them to treat their various ailments. There were a number of footpaths crossing the farm and the walkers, even in the early 1960's, were careless about closing gates, and often Monday mornings were reserved for sorting out the cattle which had wandered unhindered into silage, hay and corn fields, causing damage to the crops and time wasting rounding up and drafting. On the Monday following my conversation with Fred there were no such problems, and Mr. Chubb informed us we were, indeed, ringworming and warble-flying the cattle as Fred had predicted.

It had rained the previous day, not a heavy rain but a persistent low clouded drizzle which had saturated everything more effectively than the heaviest of thunderstorms. The fast growing corn had collected this moisture and refused to relinquish it and, though the stems were heavily bowed, the droplets stubbornly maintained their precarious hold. A mist was rising under a reluctant sun, hovering low over the fields promising a fine warm day to come.

We were to collect the cattle from a field about two miles away from the yards. Nearly everyone on the farm was involved in this cattle drive, for although Mr. Chubb's shorthorns were magnificent animals – the silver cups on his sideboard bearing witness to that – they were exceedingly wild. This added spice to the drive, but it was no help when they were in the yards. Favourite sticks were retrieved from behind cobwebbed beams in the barn where they had reposed since the last cattle drive, and we climbed aboard the trailer behind Alan's tractor. We looked a rough bunch, dressed in our oldest and most expendable clothes. Fred, his cap reversed, his ragged threadbare boiler suit that had resisted his wife's best efforts to remove the ingrained dust from the feed mill only just decent over trousers which were so riddled with holes it was difficult to detect he was wearing any at all, was anticipating the drive with an obvious relish, smiling toothlessly to himself. I noticed his underpants clearly showed through the holes in his outer clothing. He leaned slightly forward on his stick, awaiting the lurch of the trailer as we started off, looking more like a first world war aviator on his way to do battle than a farm worker setting off to confront Mr. Chubb's uncertain cattle.

'If you doesn't get them legs of the edge off the trailer, Davy, the first car that comes along'll whip 'em off an' you'll walk on your knees for the rest of your life,' Fred advised me. I took his point and stood up on the trailer like the rest.

Nearly everything in my first year as a farm student was a new experience as the seasons progressed, and Mr. Chubb's by turns excitable and stubborn cattle were no exception. I knew little about ringworm and nothing at all about warble flies and it was something of a shock to come to the field and see the cattle running down towards the gate ravaged by the irritating scabs of the ringworm, covering their faces, necks and bodies to such an extent there was, in the worst affected, little sign of any hair, leaving them looking as though they had patches of cardboard randomly pasted onto them by a child.

The warble flies were less obvious, laying their eggs on the underbellies of the cattle for the larvae to burrow their way up to the backbone, ready for flight the following year. Closer inspection revealed a series of lumps along the spine where the larvae had pierced the skin for air, at the same time ruining the hide and causing untold misery for the animal. These repulsive grubs were the size of a man's thumb. Few of the cattle were unaffected.

'They knows when they warbles comes in the summer,' Fred told me, 'they sticks their tails in the air an' takes off, charging around the fields, but the warbles always gets them in the end.'

A loud 'come on' was all that was needed for the cattle to come tearing down to the gate, and then the real work started. With only one man at the rear, technically driving them, the rest of us were either at the flanks or in front of the mob of some thirty-five shorthorn steers, determinedly charging down the road as fast as they could manage. And it was all we could manage to contain them, brandishing our sticks and, above all, running.

'Watch out, Davy, they'se going in the barley,' Fred yelled. Like an out of control train they thundered up a bank and into an unfenced field of soaking wet corn. It was my misfortune to be on this flank and I desperately charged through the saturated knee-high barley, the green stalks bending, splashing their moisture up my clothing, wetting my face and filling my boots. I needn't have bothered, for they came to a halt, blowing and panting against a fence in a bovine parody of overworked steam-engines. Quietened by their brief display of independence, they placidly allowed themselves to be driven down the road.

I was thoroughly soaked and most uncomfortable, my trousers sticking clammily and coldly to my legs, making walking a misery. As we passed Mr. Chubb's house he came down the path and saw my predicament.

'I'll bring you a pair of my trousers up to the yards presently,' he said.

' 'E'll never fit your trousers,' said Fred. 'There's more of you than there is of 'im; it'll take a tidy few of Mrs. Chubb's dinners for Davy to fill 'em out.'

'It's lucky you're not lending him a pair,' Mr. Chubb retorted. 'He would probably be arrested.'

We arrived at the yards without further mishap, Mr. Chubb bringing along the promised trousers. Fred was right, I reflected as I put them on, it would need a tidy few of Mrs. Chubb's lunches for them to ever fit me. Wilf produced a pocket knife and some binder twine and firmly tied me into them. Trimming off the ends of the twine, he remarked, 'Always carry a knife, some string an' a shilling, nipper, an' you'll not go far wrong.' It was profound advice from Wilf.

Preparations were underway in the yards. Buckets of disinfectant were placed at strategic points and James issued us with thick dark orange gloves. I have never liked wearing rubber gloves, or gloves of any kind, and told him so.

'Please yourself,' James replied. 'I caught ringworm once off the cattle. It takes weeks to clear up, itches furiously all the time and, just when you think it has gone, flares up again in a different place. It keeps you awake most of the night too,' he added ominously.

71

I rapidly changed my mind and put on the heavy rubber gloves. I looked around the yards; the cattle were rubbing their irritating scabs against the metal railings, rolling their eyes either in the agony or the ecstasy this brought. I studied Fred. He was scratching his left knee, and I watched the others. They were all surreptitiously scratching themselves, a light scratch to the arm, another to the back of the leg. Wilf repeatedly lifted his awful tartan cap and scratched his surprisingly sparse hair, scowling when he replaced the dirty headgear with a firm twist. The habit was irresistible and I soon found myself dragging my fingernails up the side of my knee. Fred had been right when he had said, 'You'll itch an' scratch all day an' all night long.'

He caught my eye. 'See what I means now, Davy boy? Worst bloody job on the farm.'

James was in charge of the operation. Mr. Chubb, Fred informed me, was well known for arranging a game of golf when we were 'ringworming and warbling'. He could hardly be blamed. He had served his time carrying out this scratchy and unpopular task, and the attraction of a round of golf did not bear comparison to curing a mob of ill-tempered, uncomfortable cattle of their parasites.

Fred took over the crush – a tubular metal contraption with a hinged bar secured by a pin – which was thrust behind the animal's head, preventing it from advancing or retreating. The bar was built into a gate, and when Fred released the pin he pulled the bar back, opened the gate and released the occupant. The race behind the crush accommodated two more steers, controlled by a heavy metal pole slotted behind their legs and rumps, cutting off escape from the rear. James, Wilf and Alan were in charge of the treatment. The rest of us itchy gang drove the reluctant cattle into the crush, shouting loudly, swearing all the time, twisting and endeavouring to avoid flailing hooves.

It was no easy task. A particularly stubborn and bloody-minded steer backed off, forcing the metal pole from my hands where it clattered and bounced on the ground, and returned to the yard.

'Open the crush, Fred,' James said, 'and let him see his way out.' We tried again and the steer, seeing unimpeded daylight at the end of the crush, roared through it, defeating Fred's fumbling reaction on the gate. Worse than that it was followed by another opportunist before Fred slammed the gate shut. The steers had to be drafted from the treated animals, frustrating us and adding time to a job we all wanted finished as soon as possible.

The crush was attached to the concreted metal uprights of the yards by heavily wound strands of binder twine. The constant movement chafed through the twine and the crush, with its terrified occupant, took off around the slippery concrete like a runaway 'bus, bouncing off the rails with dreadful clangings, scaring all of the cattle and most of us. There was pandemonium, but eventually we rescued the bolting crush and secured it more firmly to its anchorage.

Alan studiously applied cream to the ringworm scabs, vigorously rubbing it in until the scabs ruptured and bled, while James and Wilf attacked the warble fly larvae living complacently in the flesh either side of the backbone, feeding off their unwilling hosts. They worked their thumbs down either side of the fat grubs, squeezing hard and, with luck, they popped out like champagne corks and were stamped underfoot. There was an obvious knack to this. Too much pressure in the wrong place caused them to explode in the face, and to judge from Wilf's language he lacked the skill of James, as Fred continually and tactlessly reminded him.

Although I was allowed my turn popping these noxious grubs out of the steers' hides – and it was hard work on the thumbs – my place was in the yards. Besides, time was running short, and the student's turn was only a token one, to at least say he had done the job.

The yards were becoming increasingly greasy, both cattle and men sliding around on the slippery concrete, a mixture of liquified dung and mud flying up our clothing. The steers hated the job as much as we did, but to be simultaneously assaulted by warble fly larvae internally and ringworm externally must have been a torture more unbearable than a day in Mr. Chubb's cattle yards could inflict.

At last we finished. We washed our hands and arms in the buckets of disinfectant, and returned the now submissive cattle to their field, all the fight gone from them. There was no trouble on the road this time. I remarked to Fred that at least the job was behind us.

'Same as I says, you,' he replied, 'that's just the start. We's got to do 'em again in a fortnight, an' now they knows what to expect we'll 'ave a job to even shift 'em out of the field. We won't need all of us up the front next time, we'll be at the back trying to move 'em down the road. They ain't stupid you know. An' then there's all the rest of the cattle to do.' I wished I had kept quiet. And Fred's words rang through my mind that night as I tossed and turned in fitful sleep, itching and scratching all night.

෯

My father made a good choice when he persuaded Mr. Chubb to take me on as a farm student during that fateful game of golf. I had been working on his farm for several months when, at one of our weekly lunches, he announced he had made arrangements for me to join the local young farmers club. I viewed his decision with considerable suspicion, for he had announced at just such a lunch several weeks previously that he was on the panel of the Growmore Club quiz.

'I cannot go,' he said, 'and you will be taking my place. I have told the Major, who will be the quizmaster, to collect you and return you home.

It was no use protesting to Mr. Chubb my knowledge of farming was sketchy, to say the least, and I had not been on the farm for long or most of the other members of the team were at least twenty years my senior and had been in farming all their lives; I was to go, and that was all there was to it.

I was slowly becoming used to his sometimes eccentric sense of humour, and I suspected he had no valid reason for absenting himself, but rather he had told his friends he was sending his student along for a bit of fun whilst he had an evening at home with Mrs. Chubb. There was certainly no surprise when I was introduced as Mr. Chubb's replacement, but most of the questions defeated me entirely. The technicalities of the square footage allowed for poultry in deep litter houses were far beyond me, especially as there were no hens on the farm other than those the farm workers allowed to peck and scratch around in their back gardens in return for the odd egg.

ೞ

Mr. Chubb was nothing if not shrewd, and he knew by making me reluctantly join the Young Farmers Club he was opening doors to me which, in later years, would have remained firmly closed had I not done so.

'You wants to watch they young farmers, Davy,' Fred informed me. 'It's a marriage club. No good'll come of it, never 'as. They'se all stuck up an' comes round farm walks treating us like dirt. You'll end up, if you ain't careful, marrying a fat little bank clerk an' 'ave 'alf a dozen children afore ye's thirty.'

His philosophy contained an element of truth, for there were people from many different backgrounds in the club and some were, as he put it, stuck up and there were undoubtedly those who regarded it a marriage club, but Mr. Chubb knew what he was about making me join. I met new people, and not necessarily those connected with farming in any way and, more importantly, I met fellow farm students. It was from some of them I learned what I had always suspected – Mr. Chubb was a good man from whom to learn farming. Many of the more unscrupulous farmers – and there were some who not only charged their students' parents for the privilege of having their sons working on their farms but also used them as manual labourers without the slightest intention of helping them learn anything about farming at all. Mr. Chubb had the interest of his student at heart; he was more longsighted than many of his colleagues.

The Young Farmers Club met, appropriately enough, in the back room of a pub. Meetings seldom started punctually; the guest speaker was often delayed in the bar for a considerable time, which was not always helpful for the delivery of the talk. As Mr. Chubb had foreseen, I made new friends, learned a little about farming and much more about rural Hampshire and its inhabitants.

From time to time I wondered how my old public school friends were faring, but these thoughts became more fleeting as I worked my way into the beginnings of my farming career. One of them came to stay for a few days and I took him to a Young Farmers Club meeting at which the speaker was a local vet. His subject was lambing, in considerable detail, and I could see my friend paling under the onslaught.

'I like the countryside,' he condescendingly told me later, 'and your new friends have a certain curiosity value.' He paused to elaborately fill his new pipe while I patiently waited for him to continue. 'That vet fellow of yours, I didn't think it was necessary for him to go into so much gory detail.' He sat back, noisily and inexpertly sucking on his pipe. I thought he looked ridiculous.

He was wrong about the vet. Without such attention to detail my friend might well have been denied his roast lamb to eat for Sunday lunch in his modern suburban home. I was content to both work and learn my farming in the depths of the countryside, guided by Mr. Chubb and his band of amateur teachers. Even trainee stockbrokers have to eat, and my friend seemed to have his priorities reversed. He had overlooked an important fact: without the farmer his daily juggling with figures and percentages would be impossible.

I was growing away from perceived roots, and it was no bad thing.

CB

My joining the Young Farmers Club caused endless amusement to the farm workers.

'Christ,' Fred, both my mentor and my tormentor, remarked one morning after a meeting, 'you looks rough. You wants to watch they young farmers, Davy, else you'll end up with a beer belly like Wilf's an' then you won't be no good for nothing except bouncing up an' down on a tractor all day. I said all along they young farmers weren't no good for you.'

I often wondered whether there was a slight pang of jealousy sometimes. The farmworkers enjoyed their student. He unconsciously refreshed their minds, allowing them to recall the innocence of their own youth; to have him taken over by the young farmers once a week, I sensed, slightly annoyed them. I had to endeavour to steer a course that tried to please all people – no easy matter, especially as my parents entered into the conundrum.

CB

We had a young farmers scavenge hunt one summer evening. It was a car scavenge hunt and not all young farmers were as fortunate as I to have a long suffering mother who was prepared to lend her son her treasured Morris Minor for the evening. It was a popular event, and we were allowed to bring along our friends: there was the promise of a party at the end. Unfortunately, the number of cars was less than the organisers had envisaged – two per car had been the idea – and I was allocated three total strangers, two young men and a girl.

I never discovered whose friends they were, but as they were obviously separated from them, conversation proved difficult. Gradually they loosened up, and as the scavenge hunt progressed, with the prospect of the party looming closer, they became more talkative. The last item on the list, doubtless included by a committee member with a perverted sense of humour, was an envelope full of manure. I knew, I told my companions, exactly where I could find some cattle dung. By now it was almost dark, and I drove to a farm which was on the main road with the farmyard leading directly off it and, by chance, this farm was *en route* to the party.

'I won't be a moment,' I said, clutching my envelope. The heavy oak gates were closed but yielded to my push. I couldn't see a thing, for by now the darkness was overwhelming. Tentatively stepping forward my left foot suddenly sank into a soft, smelly substance and, off balance, was rapidly followed by my right foot; in all I took four involuntary strides into a pool of crusted foul smelling slurry in the centre of the yard which bubbled and belched around my knees, the hidden odours released by the disturbance. Retreating carefully from the gurgling heaving mess, the dripping stained envelope filled with slurry, I returned to the car, explaining my predicament to the astonished occupants.

'There is only one thing to do,' I said, wiping off the worst excesses from my ruined trousers with long grass plucked from the verge in the light of the headlamps, 'I will take you to my home, have a quick bath and then we'll go to the party.'

A helpful motorist pulled up and asked if he could assist. It was difficult to see how he could. Startled by my reply he hastily moved away.

We drove off in total silence. The smell was appalling, drops of slurry slowly dripping off my trousers onto the floor of the Morris Minor: it would need a thorough clean if my mother were to allow me to use it again. It was hard to imagine the thoughts of my companions, anticipating a party, but ending up trapped in a car with an evil smelling young farmer.

When we reached my home, I flung them some magazines to read and went to take my bath. Unfortunately my parents were holding a bridge party that evening. The only way to the bathroom was through the room in which they were playing. Mumbling my explanations, delicately tiptoeing barefoot over the expensive carpet, hoping the remains of the effluent clung to my trousers, I retired to the sanctuary of the bathroom. Sitting in the bath, washing the slurry from my legs, I reflected I was in for a difficult morning.

We made the party, just, and my fellow scavengers fled to find more sane company.

'Same as I says, you,' Fred remarked when I related the story the next day, 'when you goes on one of they scavenging hunts again, take a bloody torch.'

I mentally added a torch to Wilf's 'shilling, knife and piece of string'.

CR

6.

Trouble with Trimming
and Stubborn Sheep

Many of the jobs on farms could be repetitious and boring, as indeed they can be in any type of work, but farming is a profession at the mercy of the elements and tedious jobs seldom lasted long before the always fickle weather decreed a change.

One such task was trimming. Shunned by most of the others, it was the student who was landed with an ancient Fordson and a rickety Hayter trimmer that had seen better days. The work was hardly exacting, knocking the straggly seed heads off the grass to bring it on again, and time only passed slowly if it was allowed to. I rather enjoyed trimming, sitting on the old Fordson, the canvas cab with its scratched, yellowed cellophane windows flapping in the breeze like the ear warmers attached to old-fashioned hats, bumping up and down the field, wrapped up in my own world, temporarily cut off from reality, the soporific beat of the engine allowing random thoughts to wander freely around the mind. Back and forth in a forty-acre field, the narrow Hayter with its spinning blades relentlessly chopping off the seed heads, it sometimes seemed as if the trimming would never be finished, but imperceptibly the lines grew thinner and after the final turn it was almost with regret I closed the gate and set off for a new field. For a short time it was as though a part of me remained in the previous field where I had such pleasant thoughts, like the lingering memory of an enjoyable holiday. The feeling soon passed as I settled to my new territory and built up a new feeling of ambience and peace.

It was not always so peaceful. One morning Mr. Chubb instructed me to trim a notoriously steep and difficult piece of ground.

'Be careful,' he advised, 'it's very steep, and there are parts where you will not be able to go. I'll send James up later to show you.'

I drove to the field, jumped off the tractor, and surveyed it. There was a gentle slope by the entrance from the road, and a steep pull up to the top, which was a narrow ridge barely fifty yards wide. Below the ridge lay about five acres of reasonably level ground reached by a precipitous thin bank, rutted by sheep tracks, looking like a spoon with a fifty-yard handle and a five-acre end. The remainder was obviously far too steep for a tractor. It didn't seem too bad, and I started on the gentle easy slope by the road. In no time at all James roared up in his Land Rover.

'I don't know what Mr. Chubb's about sending you up here,' he said, 'It's far too dangerous for someone of your experience. You can't do those bits,' he continued, indicating the obvious. 'And leave that piece below the ridge. You could overturn the tractor just getting to it.'

He departed at full speed, releasing all his nervous energy on the clutch and throttle. Half-an-hour later he was back.

'Thought I would call in on my way to breakfast to see how you were doing,' he said. I was barely a quarter of the way up the gentle slope.

When I was almost at the top, Mr. Chubb pulled up by the gateway on his way from his post-breakfast inspection of the corn. It was one of his rituals. He lumbered up the field towards me. I stopped the tractor and, slightly out of breath, he clasped his hands over the top of the rear wheel.

'Don't take too much notice of James,' he said. 'He thinks the field worse than it is. You will have to get used to working sideling ground around here. All it needs is common sense.'

He ambled down to his Land Rover, driving down the road for his cup of coffee with Mrs. Chubb. His routine was well known.

I contemplated the almost vertical climb up to the ridge. 'Never change gear on steep ground,' Wilf had told me. 'If you runs out of revs you'se 'ad it, an' you'll slide backwards faster an' faster an' tangle up with whatever's on the back of your tractor.'

I chose a suitably low gear, ascended to the top of the ridge without trouble and started trimming the fifty yard by about four hundred yard strip of grass. It was a beautiful day, the sun beating down, the canvas of the cab tied back to the thin metal bars of its frame and the doors tied open with baler twine to the bonnet catches, the Hayter trimmer humming peacefully behind the tractor. James had not made his intrusive hourly visit – perhaps he was learning some of Mr. Chubb's common sense – and the views from either side of the ridge were magnificent. Far below me, across the valley on a neighbouring farm, was a tiny tractor engaged on the same task as me. The vistas stretched to infinity; it was my world up there and nothing else mattered for every problem had become miniaturised and inconsequential. I burst into unmelodious song at the sheer exhilaration of the place; after all, there was no one to hear, and it was my world alone. Still in good voice I descended the precipitous track and trimmed the five acres below the ridge. When I had finished a relieved James directed me to my new field.

'It's all straight up and down work,' he said, 'no sideling ground. You won't have any problems there.'

Several days later, at the local pub, a man came over to me. He proved to be the driver of the tiny tractor I had observed across the valley.

'You was singing well trimming that 'ill of Mr. Chubb's the other day,' he said. 'Very near deafened me when I stopped for my tea.'

He returned to his friends with a smile and a twinkle in his eyes. I had no idea how the sound must have carried. I was mortified. It really had not been my world at all.

ଔ

I viewed my next field with horror. It was about thirty-five acres and, as James had intimated, all straight up and down work. He had neglected to mention it was straight up hill and down hill work. The field was bisected by a valley – this farm seemed full of valleys – and it was steep, far steeper than my previous field. I decided to attack the valley first, to put it behind me so I could enjoy the ease of the level ground later. I started at the shallow end, and the further I progressed the steeper the slope became. James, I thought, must be mad to expect me to cut all of this, but he had told me it was perfectly safe when he first came to check on me.

'You won't have any trouble,' he said, 'we worked it quite safely last year.'

So I persevered, alternately looking down to the narrow floor of the valley, my backside threatening to leave the seat at any moment, or admired the clouds which appeared in line with the bonnet of the tractor as I went up the other side. The inevitable happened on one of my downhill excursions, trimming my way along the increasingly steep ground. The rear wheels lost adhesion on the slippery grass – it was fortunate it was a downhill run – and the tractor, with the wheels alarmingly appearing to rotate backwards, either a trick of the eyes or a trick of the differential, plunged at breakneck speed to the valley floor. I opened the throttle as far as it would go and tried to steer a straight line as the out of control machine, hell-belt on defying my attempts to master it, alternately lifting one rear wheel off the ground, then the other, tore down the hill. I safely reached level ground and jumped off the tractor to recover for a minute. There were impressive skid marks in the grass reaching back about seventy-five yards up the hill, and I considered myself fortunate to have survived the experience as I recalled James's words: 'You won't have any problems there.'

James came to check my progress a few hours later. I was trimming the flat ground above the lethal valley.

'Why have you left half the sides over there uncut?' he asked. I explained, showing him the skid marks of my near disaster. He was unconvinced.

'We managed last year when we ploughed and drilled it,' he said. 'Perhaps the grass was wet. Try again when the sun has been on it for a while longer.'

I had no intention of trying again, and I left it. James never passed any further comment, and later I asked Alan if it was true this ground had been ploughed and drilled the year before.

'We ploughed it, down'ill only, mind, with the ordinary tractor,' he confirmed. 'The plough acts like a brake, see, an' it were easy. All the cultivation an' drilling were done with the crawler.'

For all the concern James had shown for my wellbeing trimming my first steep field, he had overlooked the danger of the second. Mr. Chubb was right, all it needed was common sense and I sometimes wondered, with James, who was teaching who.

C8

Common sense was in short supply when Mr. Chubb sent me down to trim the old water meadows. These ancient pastures by the river consisted of a series of shallow ditches and sluices which, using the water from the river and by careful control of the sluices, could flood either the whole or part of the meadows, thus ensuring grazing in times of drought. Years of disuse and neglect and countless cattle's hooves had rounded the tops into the bottoms of the ditches, making them mere shallow depressions in ground, and all that remained of the sluices were piles of broken bricks and some rusty iron.

'Be sure to drive up and down the lines of the channels, and not across them,' Mr. Chubb told me.

I inspected the water meadows when I had closed the gate. It would be much quicker to go across the ditches than up and down them. I decided to ignore Mr. Chubb's advice and trim the water meadows my way.

C8

It was one of those summer days that remain locked in the memory and exaggerated by time, one of the summer days we think we have no more, the mind conveniently erasing the sweaty discomforts, the irritating insects, the overbearing humidity and retaining bright images of a perfection which exists only in the imagination.

The reality of that day in the water meadows was the desiccating sun, case hardening the dry stems of the seed-bearing grass I was trimming, the heat haze and the flies: the flies that rose in a buzzing swarm from the steaming liquid cow pats as the tractor squelched through them seconds later – Mr. Chubb's steers were in these meadows – and the smell of wet

81

dung clinging to the wheels, falling in a rain of soft brown drops on the mudguards. And the horse flies – stouts they were called locally – settling soundlessly on my arm, biting and departing almost before I was aware of them, and the clouds of flies pestering the cattle, crawling around their nostrils, into the corners of their eyes and even into their ears, the swishing of their tails, the irritated flick of their heads and twitching of their ears not deterring them for a moment.

I swooped and dived over the well rounded ditches and the cattle, now the novelty of my entrance had faded, continued their interrupted grazing and their ceaseless battle with the flies; the tractor almost drove itself, the up and down motion reminiscent of sailing on a gentle swell. I lapsed into a somnolent day dream, only emerging from it to turn the tractor at the ends of the meadow.

Suddenly the tractor stopped dead. I pitched forward over the steering wheel, wondering for a second what had happened. The engine was running normally but the machine was stationary, the wheels clawing at air. It had grounded on one of the deeper ditches. No wonder Mr. Chubb had advised me to go up and down those innocent looking mounds. I cursed him for not giving me the reason, but that was his way and I suspected he had anticipated exactly the outcome of my excursion into the water meadows.

It was imperative I extracted the tractor from the ditch before he drove up to the gate in his Land Rover. It was not an easy task. For a start the ever-curious steers with their attendant flies had sensed some fun to liven up their day and were already standing round the stranded Fordson awaiting developments. There were plenty of bricks from the decayed sluices and, forcing my way through the cattle, I brought piles of them back, hitting them under the back wheels with my fist. The cattle moved closer to gain a better view. It was becoming increasingly hot, and their flies willingly transferred themselves to my eyes, ears, face and nostrils. I tried driving the steers away, but it was hopeless for they immediately reformed. They weren't going to miss this for anything.

As soon as I released the clutch the bricks spun out from under the wheels, temporarily removing my onlookers, but hardly solving my problem. There was a heavy hammer in the toolbox and I used this to ram the bricks more firmly under the wheels, without effect. The tyres spat the bricks out with contemptuous ease.

Pouring sweat, covered in flies, furious with the cattle and anticipating the imminent arrival of Mr. Chubb, I studied the drawbar, which was firmly embedded in the earth. There were three settings on this, for lowering or raising it and the settings were secured by heavy duty pins on either side.

The drawbar was on its lowest mark, and I reasoned if I could hit the pins out with the heavy hammer the tractor would drop back to the ground. It was difficult, bent over, half-blinded by sweat dripping stingingly into my eyes, my backside constantly licked by rough, inquisitive tongues but, at last, with a resounding bang which drove my bovine companions half way up the field, I succeeded and the tractor was once again on an even keel.

The relief was enormous; there was no sign of Mr. Chubb and I demurely resumed my trimming up and down the channels as he had told me to do in the first place, the breeze on my face from the speed of the tractor dispersing most of the flies and drying the sweat.

Half-an-hour later Mr. Chubb's Land Rover came into view.

'How are you getting on,' he enquired. 'Any problems?'

'None at all, Mr. Chubb,' I replied.

'Fine bunch of steers,' he said, pointing at them with his stick. 'Some of the best we have ever reared on this estate. I shouldn't be surprised to see them top the market when I send them off.'

I often wondered at his sense of humour and I half thought I had got away with my misdemeanour, but nemesis arrived from an unexpected direction.

ೞ

Enjoying a pint in the pub a few days later, I was tapped on the shoulder by a gnarled old finger. I turned and looked into the watery light blue eyes of Stanley, the octogenarian semi-retired gamekeeper, bow-legged, wearing gaiters above his boots, worn trousers, the inevitable collarless shirt covered by a waistcoat and an old trilby hat. He leant on his stick.

'You 'ad yerself in a fine mess down they water medders,' he said. 'Ain't laughed so much for years.'

'Where were you?' I asked him.

He chuckled deeply, drawing on his pint.

'I were in they trees,' he replied. 'Twere dark in there an' you couldn't see I. I daresn't reckon Mr. Chubb'd be best pleased if 'ee knew. You'd best buy I a pint of mild an' we'll call it square.'

I bought him two.

ೞ

Mr. Chubb's shorthorn cattle were some of the best in the county. Years of careful breeding, prudent selection of bulls and what Mr. Chubb termed 'a good eye' had earned him the reputation of the best cattle breeder in the area.

'Buyers come from miles away to purchase my cattle,' he told me immodestly. 'When they see my name on the catalogue, they thrust their hands deeper into their pockets than they will for any other farmers' animals.'

He had handed most of the responsibility for the shorthorns to James, maintaining at his age he was too old to work properly with them, concentrating on the less demanding and much less interesting corn. The shorthorns, however, always remained 'his' and James was never permitted to take any decisions without Mr. Chubb's approval.

'He's too young, yet,' I heard him tell Fred one day. 'In another ten years, if he listens to me, he will become a good cattle man.'

Sheep he regarded as a necessary nuisance, a part of the traditional farming rotation, fertilising the soil, supplementing the farm's income with lambs and wool, but requiring endless attention which was not always accorded them at busy times. As a result they tended to suffer, especially from foot-rot, which was an eternal problem with sheep. In between the more important jobs such as silaging and haymaking we would make an all out attempt to tidy up the unfortunate flock, paring their feet, cutting out the foot-rot that so afflicted them and running them through the powerful formaldehyde footbath. This treatment was supposed to be repeated the following week but seldom was as something more important usually intervened and the sheep were forgotten by all except Alan. It became a constant battle to keep their feet in proper trim.

❧

Alan had built the sheep pens under some oak trees adjoining the lane, two miles from the farm, and oak trees and sheep, on a hot day, were strong attractors of horseflies. As we were also looking for maggots – nature was as cruel to sheep with maggots as she was to cattle with warble flies – we had aerosol tins of maggot spray to hand, and before we started all headgear was sprayed with the evil smelling liquid. This was supposed to deter the horseflies.

'Best put some on Davy's 'air, seein' 'ee's not wearing no 'at,' said Fred with a dangerous glint in his eyes. I hastily backed off, for I would not have put anything past Fred.

We ran the ewes through the pens – the lambs had been weaned a few weeks before – picking out the many lame ewes, tipping them with a knee to the rump and a deft flick of the hand under the jaw. When their feet had been pared, their bodies checked for maggots, they were turned into a holding pen to await their turn through the footbath.

I worked with Luke, a merry rotund man in his early sixties whose trade mark was a large green beret almost too large for his head. His bright eyes were nearly hidden in the spreading creases of the laughter lines fanning out around them, and he talked ceaselessly, partly to me, partly to himself and often to the sheep.

'A little bit over that way, girl, that's it, an' we'll soon 'ave you done. That's my girl, hold steady there an' let I whip that bit off quick. She's done now, Davy, let's 'ave another 'un.' (They all called me Davy by now: I had given up the fight). Some says good old Luke, others speaks the truth.'

He slowly straightened, creaking alarmingly. I had noticed his tendency to creak before, and Luke must have noticed my puzzlement.

'Don't you worry about they noises, Davy,' he said. 'It's not me bones, only me corsets. Most of us old 'uns wears 'em, it 'olds us together. We'd fall apart without 'em.'

He chuckled and whistled a little tune as I brought him the next ewe.

'I doesn't know much about sheep,' he said. 'I'm what they calls manual. Mostly I goes fencing, 'anging gates, diggin' 'oles, pickin' 'taters. You name it, I does it. Some says good old Luke, others speaks the truth.' He bent, creaking, to his task.

I could see he was no expert with the lambsfoot knife, his blood freely mixing with that of the sheep. It was a notoriously bad area for tetanus – Mr. Chubb had insisted I was immunised before I started working for him and I asked Luke whether he had had his tetanus injections.

'Never 'ad one in my life,' he replied. 'Never been to the doctor neither, not since I were a nipper with croup. Ain't never smoked since.' He chuckled to himself.

I believed him, too, though how he had never contracted tetanus, let alone some horrible blood disease from the sheep remained a mystery. Luke was always a picture of good health, but his hands were a mass of scars mostly from barbed wire, for we did not wear protective gloves in those days, and from the self-inflicted wounds from the razor-sharp lambsfoot knife.

We ran the first batch of sheep through the eye-watering, nose-stinging, astringent formaldehyde footbath, and sat down under the trees to have our lunch. We seldom took our lunch with us, but as we were so far away from the farm it had hardly been worth returning. Mr. Chubb had forewarned us the previous day, and my mother had cut me some of her slim 'bridge party' sandwiches: the farmworkers' wives had prepared the brick-sized sandwiches their men enjoyed.

'If we only takes an' 'alf hour for our dinner, we can knock off early,' said Wilf, always the opportunist.

'We'll take our hour, you, an' enjoy it,' Fred replied firmly.

And enjoy it we did. It was peaceful in that lonely place, the hot sun beating down on the browned grass. It had not rained for weeks. Scarcely a car came down the lane all day; civilisation was a remote memory. The ewes stood patiently in the yards, flicking their ears and occasionally stamping their feet in an attempt to ward off the flies, all the time chewing their cuds, pausing with a dreamy look in their eyes while one piece was swallowed and the next rippled up their gullets, before resuming their leisurely task. We munched our sandwiches, and most of the farmworkers drank their tea, poured black from their flasks into the flask tops, the milk added from a small bottle secreted in their lunch bags. 'It don't taste right if the milk's added when you makes it,' Wilf had told me. 'It's best to add the milk separate.' I preferred lemonade. 'Makes you more thirsty when you'se working,' Fred told me. 'You drinks more an' more of it an' ends up running to the 'edge every five minutes. You ought to 'ave tea like the rest of us.'

It was timeless, this place, like so many other parts of the farm. I had noticed what appeared to be ancient ditches dug around the edge of the field, quite unlike those in the water meadows, the spoil thrown out to form a rough bank which was colonised by ash trees. I asked Alan what they were, and he told me they were made to mark the boundaries of farms centuries ago. I marvelled at the work involved excavating these earthworks, wondering how those bygone labourers would have enjoyed their lunch hours. Apart from the thermos flasks and the tractor parked in the corner, the scene was probably little different from all those hundreds of years ago when the boundaries were thrown up like ramparts.

The hour was up, and we slowly, reluctantly returned to work. I was not the only one affected by the tranquillity of the surroundings. At four o'clock we finished paring the last sheep's feet and prepared to run the final batch through the footbath. For some reason the ewes turned stubborn and bloody-minded, refusing to run through the bath, baulking at the entrance which was blocked by sheep standing in the muddy formaldehyde solution. Perhaps, having spent the day in the yards against their will, they were getting their own back. I could hardly blame them.

' 'Ere, Luke,' shouted Fred, 'get down by that bloody bath an' prod 'em through.'

Luke stiffly ambled down and, leaning over the rails, 'prodded' them through. The ewes, abandoning their protest, funnelled through the foot bath like sand running through an hour-glass, smoothly moving into the holding pen beyond. Luke remained bent over the rails, watching them. After a while, they blocked again. Luke made no attempt to move them on.

'Give 'em a shove up, Luke,' Fred yelled. Luke did not respond. 'What's wrong with the bugger?' Fred asked in exasperation. ' 'Ee gone bloody deaf?'

'Asleep, more like,' said Alan. 'I'll give 'im an' 'and.'

Alan went over to Luke and shook him. Very slowly, like a sawn tree just starting to fall, with all the attendant creaking, Luke gently slid down the railings, landing flat on his back in the grass. He didn't move.

''Ee's dead,' shrieked a panic-stricken Alan. We all rushed to Alan's side and stood, looking down at Luke's prostrate form.

' 'Ee ain't never dead,' said Fred, taking off his cap and vigorously fanning the air in front of Luke's face. Luke groaned and opened his eyes. Fred continued fanning the air.

'Same as I says, you, it's they formalin fumes what done it,' he said. ''Ee's only passed out.'

Luke ponderously sat up and surveyed us.

'Some says good old Luke,' he said, 'others speaks the truth.'

ᗩ

7.

A Little Roughing and a Rough Show for the Student

Bob came to work for Mr. Chubb in the late 1920's. He was an inoffensive man of medium height with distinctive purple lips. He was slow of speech and thought: in fact he was slow in everything he did. He had been driving the farm's International crawler tractor for as long as anyone could remember, and it was debatable whether he had always been slow or whether years of driving the lumbering crawler had slowed him both mentally and physically.

The seasons had taken their toll, and hunched over the controls of his tractor in the narrow confines of the thin metal cab, he had developed a pronounced stoop. His scraggy, creased neck emerged from the generous opening of his outsize boiler suit, and his square head, topped with a flat cap, completed the illusion of a tortoise. He was disliked by all his fellow farm workers and was contemptuously referred to as 'Pal'. When he came to the farm all those years ago, he called everyone 'Pal' and the sobriquet became his own nickname, following him to the grave.

I tackled Fred about him one day.

'Same as I says, you, 'ee's a lazy bugger an' always 'as been,' he said. 'When 'ee first came 'ere an' started calling us all 'Pal', that done it. We's all got names an' we uses them; we's not all called 'Pal', so we turned the tables on 'un and started calling 'im Pal. That cured 'im, an' 'ee's bin called Pal ever since. 'Ee's from the smoky country we reckons.'

The allusion to Gipsy origins was probably unfair, but farmworkers were deeply suspicious of Gipsies and, deep down, were frightened of them, although they would never admit to it. His standing was not enhanced by his son moving into the scrap metal business, and when most of the brass tap fittings around the farm disappeared one weekend, Fred was in no doubt as to who had taken them.

Pal lived a lonely life, both in the village and on his crawler tractor. The farm cottage in which he lived was the most remote on the estate, and he never socialised in the pub with his colleagues. Throughout the winter he was never seen in the farmyard in the mornings when Mr. Chubb issued his orders for the day and where we all had a contact before we departed for our various tasks. Nor did he appear at lunchtime when we all returned to the yard, and again, on dark winter evenings there was never a sign of him. Pal spent his winter ploughing.

As soon as harvest was completed he started his winter ploughing, working from field to field, week in, week out, month after month. We saw him on Friday afternoons at the farm office when we collected our wages from the Major and sometimes we caught a glimpse of him ploughing his solitary way across a frosty landscape in his red tractor when we were on our way to other jobs on the farm. Mr. Chubb told me he tried to make a point of seeing him every day but, he admitted, he sometimes forgot about Pal for days on end and was only reminded of him when he knocked on his door in the evening asking for some more diesel to be brought out. I was often detailed to do this, filling one of the farm's two diesel 'bombs' – so called for that is what they resembled – with about fifty gallons of fuel and towing the bomb to wherever Pal happened to be, and then returning with the empty bomb later.

Entering the field, I would unhitch the full bomb and attach the empty one to my tractor. All Pal's equipment was left by the gate, his cans of grease and engine oil, the funnel for the diesel and the two-gallon pourer all neatly arranged alongside the hedge, and his ancient bicycle was carefully leant against it. This bicycle was the reason we hardly ever saw him in the winter, for he left home in the morning and cycled directly to where he had left off the previous evening, returning home on it some nine hours later through the darkened lanes.

Moving fields must have taken hours. All the cans, spare ploughshares, tools and other equipment were laboriously distributed both on the crawler and the four-furrowed trailed plough. The diesel bomb was attached to the end of the plough and, finally, Pal's bicycle was firmly tied to the back of the cab with binder twine, the whole process being reversed when the new field was reached – sometimes only a few hundred yards away. Pal was the very antithesis of modern rush and tear, but his winter ploughing was always completed on time, and it was always done well. Bumping across corn fields at harvest time, it was easy to tell which fields the rough and ready Wilf had ploughed, and the smooth, even ones to which Pal had expertly applied his craft.

Often, when I arrived with the bomb, Pal would climb stiffly out of his crawler and lumber over for a chat. First he would take out a battered tin that had once contained cough drops, and carefully open it. Inside, protected by layers of cotton wool, was his pocket watch which he placed in the palm of his hand and studied intently. When the position of the hands were clear to him, he returned it to the tin and thrust it back into the depths of his pocket. Next, another tin was taken out of his other trouser pocket, his tobacco tin. Removing a cigarette paper and placing it on his lower lip, he would start talking, the paper fluttering up and down on his lip as he spoke. The loneliness of his job and the paucity of human contact opened the floodgates of his thoughts, and once he had started it was difficult to escape from him.

'I may be wrong, but I know I'm right' was always his preface before launching into rambling opinions of the weather, the state of farming or the anticipated breakdown of his tractor. While he talked he went through the ritual of manufacturing his cigarette, the paper still firmly attached to his lower lip. He used pipe tobacco, maintaining it gave him a better smoke and it was also cheaper than cigarette tobacco, he informed me. He laboriously extracted the strands from his tin, replacing some and then taking a few more out until he judged he had the exact amount for the perfect cigarette and, placing the wodge of tobacco between his hands he rhythmically rolled it around until it reached the required consistency, all the time talking in his measured tones. 'I may be wrong, but I know I'm right.' The refrain rang in my ears for hours after.

Moistening his lip, he at last removed the hypnotic paper and started to roll his cigarette and, as another thought occurred to him he would pause, the rolled cigarette held between thumb and forefinger in mid-air, only awaiting a quick lick from his tongue, and embark upon another lengthy dissertation.

'I may be wrong, but I know I'm right…' I used to become desperate, willing him to lick the paper. But worse was to follow, for when the completed cigarette was finally placed between his lips, and he had eventually located his box of matches – always in the last of the many pockets he tried – and had clumsily extracted a match and slowly closed the box, he would pause, the match in his fingers hovering over the box like a cobra waiting to strike. And when it was struck, Pal embarked on another story, the match burning unheeded until it scorched his fingers. This mesmeric performance was repeated several times before the flame ignited his elaborately rolled cigarette, and left me feeling exhausted.

He was lonely, and the performance was calculated to spin out my visit for as long as possible, but I understood why it was always the student who supplied Pal with the diesel.

છ

'Where you bin?' demanded Fred one day after I had had a lengthy session with Pal. He had been waiting for me to return and take out the feed rations for the calves.

'You wants to do what they others does,' he continued. I innocently asked him what that was.

'They goes up to the field where Pal's ploughing,' he said, an' watches 'im through the 'edge. When 'ee turns on the 'eadland, they waits a while an' then nips in quick an' changes the bombs over.'

I thought this was mean as I felt sorry for Pal, but it was a trial listening to him, and the next time I took the bomb out to him I followed Fred's advice, and guiltily watched him through the hedge until he was out of range before I changed the bombs. The guilt persisted all day, and I resolved, in future, to let Pal have his yarn. After all, I was only the student; the others had worked with him for more than thirty years and were entitled to their opinions, although I suspected they were based on tenuous prejudice.

I think the truth was that Pal had got off to a bad start thirty years ago simply by calling everyone 'Pal', and he had never been able to redeem himself. He was rather like an unpopular boy at school when, for no apparent reason, he was 'ganged up' on, and the only difference with Pal was that he had endured it for most of his life.

ও

92

The snow came in February, small hard flakes of penetrating driving snow blown in on a freezing east wind. It was so cold that as I struggled to work in my mother's old Morris Minor, wearing several sweaters and a thick scarf, for there was no heater in the car, I saw the milk lorry, laden with churns, halted by the side of the road. The driver was lighting newspapers underneath it in an attempt to thaw the frozen diesel in the fuel lines, and I wondered if he had the refinement of a heater in his cab. Probably not, I thought. The brown flat-bed lorry was considerably older than my mother's car and in any case the question was academic as the engine was immobile. I inwardly sympathised with the driver and, slightly late, pulled into the farmyard.

Mr. Chubb, who seemed to be enjoying the cold weather, sent Fred, Pal, Wilf and myself to feed the cattle on top of the hill, the same hill where his cattle thrived so well. The snow was laying fast now, and the track up the hill was covered by several inches. Pal's ploughing had come to a halt; indeed, he told me, the tracks of his machine were frozen solid and nothing short of a blowlamp and a sledgehammer would free them.

'You drive the tractor,' Wilf ordered Pal, and he meekly obeyed – even though it was Wilf's tractor. We loaded up the feed and climbed onto the trailer. Pal slowly drove to the foot of the hill, where he stopped and looked round at us.

'Will us get up that 'ill?' He enquired.

'You should know,' Fred answered, 'You'se bin driving tractors longer than most. 'Ere, we'll jump off an' lighten the load.'

Pal let out the clutch and the Fordson started to climb the slippery track.

' 'Ee'll never get up there with a wheeled tractor,' said Wilf. 'Stupid to try.'

'Then why did you let him?' I asked, knowing very well now why he was so eager to let Pal drive his tractor.

'Because 'ee's stupid,' said Wilf. ''Ee don't know 'ow to drive a wheeled tractor; 'ee thinks 'ee's on 'is crawler an' can go anywhere. Ee's got to find out 'ee cain't.'

We watched Pal inching his way up the hill, and soon he got into difficulties, the tractor finishing up slewed across the slope, the trailer buried in the fence. Pal climbed off the tractor and, lifting his cap to scratch his head, looked at the tangle he had created.

' 'Ee'll 'ave to get a blowlamp an' sledge an' free the tracks on 'is crawler now,' said Wilf heartlessly. Crawler's the only thing that'll shift that now. ''Ee's stupid, always 'as bin.'

When James came back from his breakfast, we borrowed his Land Rover and trailer, transhipped the bags and drove up through the field to feed the cattle. From the top of the hill I could see Pal, a tiny bent figure far below us, trudging his solitary way through the snow to his crawler, a sledgehammer over his shoulder and a blowlamp in his hand.

۞

In the spring Pal cultivated the steep banks on the farm that were unsuitable for wheeled tractors often, for the drilling, teaming up with Frank, who was one of the few men on the farm who bore Pal no grudge. Pal knew these steep banks like no-one else, and at harvest time the farm's cranky, temperamental bagging combine was towed behind his crawler with Frank expertly tying the bags and tipping them onto the ground for later collection, no easy task considering the often acute angles he had to work at, with the old combine hanging down the hill trying to pull the crawler with it. I often watched Pal and Frank from the distance as they harvested the corn from the thin soil of the chalk downlands, tacking through a sea of rippling barley like a yacht crossing the ocean against the wind.

After the silaging was finished, where Pal had used his crawler to bed down the grass – Alan using the spare crawler to help – there was little call for his clumsy machine until the start of harvest. Most of the farm workers took their holidays at this time (Fred once took his family to the Isle of Wight, and I often wondered what the islanders made of him) and Pal would fill in, driving the vacant Fordsons for the fortnights.

Dung cart was a perennial summer chore, clearing out the yards where the cattle had been in-wintered, tipping the steaming loads into heaps in the fields where it was to be spread later on.

Mr. Chubb decided a week's dung cart was in order and Pal, myself, Alan and Brian were earmarked for the job. Wilf, inevitably, was in charge of loading. He firmly impressed upon me that while he was loading my trailer I was expected to clear the dung from the awkward corners where his dung fork was unable to reach, and Alan, Brian and I, using the 'four-grained prong' always obliged.

Pal was not a good driver of a wheeled tractor, as Wilf had observed. He tended to think he was driving his slow crawler and drove at about half throttle, as if he was frightened of the unaccustomed speed. He was in front of me in the rotation and I constantly caught him up, he and I often arriving for Wilf to load at the same time. He never attached himself to the four-grained prong, preferring to sit in his cab, drinking a cup of tea from his thermos flask, bent over the steering wheel, the cup placed by the side of it. This infuriated Wilf.

'Look at 'im,' he said as I returned just behind Pal. He was in position for loading, his back to Wilf and his cup of tea steaming on the diesel tank beside the steering wheel. 'I'll shift 'im out of 'is cab, you watch.'

I did. Wilf, his tractor running at maximum revs, charged the dung and lifted a great mass of it on the dung fork. With a horrible crunch of gears he roared backwards, the wheels spinning wildly on the slippery concrete, and, further straining the long suffering gearbox, he charged at Pal's trailer, looking like an ancient mariner with his unkempt dark beard, his face suffused with rage. At the last minute he slammed on the brakes, the wheels locked and he crashed into the side of the trailer. Pal's tea went flying in the air and he made a vain attempt to catch the plastic thermos cup which landed upside down on the dung caked footplate.

Wilf was right. He shifted him out of his cab, but not to the four-grained prong as he had hoped. Thereafter, as soon as Pal had positioned his tractor, he clambered out of his cab and drank his tea sitting on a low concrete wall. He was not the only one learning on this estate.

I was in a hurry one lunchtime during dung carting. We were running a little late and I was worried I wouldn't be able to get home in time to place the lunchtime bets. Rounding a corner in the deeply sunken lane, I was horrified to see Pal in front of me, driving at his usual sedentary speed. There was no escape, so I gently eased my tractor into the back of his trailer and opened the throttle, pushing him down the road at a vastly increased speed. The effect on Pal was startling: he took his hands off the steering wheel for a moment and fiddled with the hand throttle, and then he leant backwards as if the tractor was about to take flight, firmly gripping the wheel and, in turn, lifted his left foot up and then his right, examining each closely as though it might explain the sudden increase in speed. Whether he thought his tractor was possessed by a demon or not I shall never know, for Pal never mentioned the incident, and he did not once think to look behind. Resigned to his fate, he leant over the steering wheel, his nose nearly touching the windscreen. When we had almost reached the farmyard I gently eased back, and Pal visibly relaxed. He parked the tractor and nonchalantly bicycled up the road for his lunch as though nothing had happened.

When I told Fred he snorted dismissively.

'Same as I says, you, 'ee's a lazy bugger, too tired to turn round. As you got them bets on?'

I had.

☙

Roughing, or pulling wild oats from the corn by hand, was the most boring and mind-destroying job it has ever been my misfortune to perform.

Never did time pass more slowly, never was the wrist watch consulted more frequently, and never was the sky studied more closely for evidence of welcoming clouds that might bring rain and free me from this purgatory.

I told Mr. Chubb what I thought of roughing, and he was amused. 'You might not learn much about farming pulling up wild oats,' he told me, 'but it will make you appreciate the better jobs all the more.'

In truth, wild oats were not a severe problem on the farm, and it was only when there was little else to do that we were deployed on this unpopular task. Mr. Chubb sent four of us, Harry, Wilf, Jack and myself to one of the worst affected fields, and we reluctantly set off, standing in the link box mounted on the rear of Harry's tractor. Jack was the man who had taken a fatherly interest in me when I started on the farm: I had seen little of him since.

'Only four more hours an' then it's dinner time,' said Wilf gloomily as we trudged unwillingly up and down the drills, the whispering corn lightly brushing our trousers, pulling the wild oat plants out of the ground, twisting them around our wrists and pushing them into a sack for later incineration.

'Why don't Fred never do jobs like this?' Wilf continued. ''Ee's always stuck in 'is feed mill with 'is cats. Never sees 'im roughing. 'Ee thinks 'ee's foreman or something.'

'Well, 'ee is unofficial foreman,' said Jack, 'and besides 'ee's done 'is share of jobs like this. Someone's got to mix the feed. You're always moaning, Wilf – if you were in the feed mill you'd want to be away from all the dust and noise and out in the fresh air doing a nice easy job like this.'

Jack was a tall, thin man, another of Mr. Chubb's old retainers. His merry blue eyes revealed a lively sense of humour and a keen intelligence. He was a man of strong opinions with an unshakeable faith in himself, and he would stand no nonsense from anyone, least of all from Mr. Chubb. He had been sacked and reinstated more times than anyone could remember, and Mr. Chubb held him in grudging respect.

'That Dingwell (he always referred to his by his surname) has been with me for well over thirty years now,' he once told me. 'He's bloody-minded and obstinate, but I wouldn't be without him. Don't you go telling him that,' he added hastily.

He was a Londoner, and proud of it, and he was the only man on the farm not to have been born locally. Anyone with less strength of character than Jack would have found this an insurmountable hurdle in the close society of a rural setting, but he overcame the apparent handicap with ease, his no nonsense approach earning him the respect of his fellow farm workers.

Jack could 'yarn', and he could yarn effortlessly all day long if required, always entertainingly, always interestingly and without repetition, his opinions and philosophy startlingly original for someone who, in the early 1960's, was considered 'only' a farmhand. As new blood on the farm I became the focus of his intellectual attention, for a farm student who had been to public school was a challenge which appealed to Jack, and he constantly tried – and succeeded – in catching me out, to his enormous satisfaction.

We must have looked a strange quartet trudging along those lines of barley, Jack brightly talking, mostly to me, Wilf morosely chewing a match and Harry completely silent, daydreaming, mechanically thrusting the wild oats into his sack. Suddenly Jack stopped. 'Where's Harry?' he said. We turned round, and there he was, twenty yards down the field, lying flat on his face. I moved instinctively to go to him, but Wilf placed a restraining hand on my arm.

'Leave 'im be, nipper,' he said. ' 'Ee'll be all right in a moment. It's the war,' he explained. ' 'Ee ain't been the same since 'ee came back. 'Ee 'as these blackouts, but 'ee soon gets over 'em.'

Soon Harry stirred, lifted himself up on his arms as though he was doing a press-up, retrieved his spectacles which were intact and walked the twenty yards towards us, pulling wild oats as he came. He didn't say a word, and we resumed our roughing down the field as though nothing had happened. I was suspicious of Harry's blackouts – and I witnessed several of them – for he always looked perfectly normal when he regained consciousness and appeared to suffer no ill-effects from them, but maybe this, too, was a symptom of shell shock. On the other hand his lusty love life in the village, and beyond, confounded this theory in my mind. Harry's distinct if ugly features were reproduced faithfully in the young daughter of a widow a few farm cottages away from his own and I was astonished to see a teenage version of him drinking beer in a pub several villages away one evening. Maybe it was more than the war that caused his blackouts, and I whispered as much to Jack, who reacted with shock.

'There are certain things we do not talk about on this farm,' he reprimanded me, 'and that is one of them.'

Harry had never married, but he had undoubtedly sown his wild oats.

೮೪

On the way back to the farm, standing in the link box with Jack and Wilf, I hoped Harry remained conscious for the journey and I anxiously watched the back of his head, topped by a greasy felt hat, for signs of it slumping forward on his chest. I needn't have worried, and we safely pulled into the yard on the stroke of five o'clock. Harry parked his tractor in the barn, lowered the link box to the ground, collected his lunch bag from a hook on the side of the cab and walked off home without a word.

We roughed for four days, and before we had started on the morning of the fifth day, as we were taking an unscheduled break on the headland, James surprised us, driving his Land Rover unheard up the lane. Guiltily we rose to our feet, but James ignored our inactivity. The steers had broken out of their field and were wandering down the lane, grazing the verges. Relieved, and anticipating the prospect of a lively cattle drive, four reluctant roughers re-entered the real world of farming.

I never pulled a wild oat again, not on Mr. Chubb's farm nor any other I worked on – sprays have taken care of them now, and a reduced labour force – but those four days that had felt like four weeks seemed, in hindsight, ephemeral, a lost four days from an age where time ceased to matter and we were lost in time itself. Paradoxically, I often look back on my brief period of roughing from an artificial platform of frenetic modern living, recalling it almost with affection until I think more deeply and remember the utter boredom.

At least I had companionship; Pal spent nearly all the winter on his crawler tractor ploughing the downs in confined solitude.

ෆ

It was difficult for a student to learn dairying – or milking as Mr. Chubb termed it. The cowman, Norman, and his relief cowman Henry, were regarded as a breed apart from the rest of the farmworkers.

'Same as I says, you, they's lazy,' Fred informed me. 'They's paid more than us, an' in 'aying an' 'arvest they picks up overtime they's no right to.'

I encountered this prejudice towards cowmen on many farms, but Fred, as usual, carried his prejudice to extremes. He made sure the feed was taken to the dairy in the middle of milking, seeing the trailer back with loudly shouted instructions. Norman, a short quick-tempered man, inevitably emerged from his dairy in a rage, almost tripping over his long rubber apron, and a heated argument would ensue, Fred imperturbably maintaining, 'We was only bringing the feed. They cows of yourn 'ave to eat, else you wouldn't 'ave no milk, an' if you didn't 'ave no milk you wouldn't 'ave no bonus.'

It was the bonus that really infuriated Fred, a bonus, he told me, which was based on yield, and the delivery of the feed, with all the attendant noise, was calculated to upset the cows and reduce the yield.

'They doesn't like the noise an' they doesn't like strangers,' Fred told me, an' they gives less milk.'

Even Mr. Chubb had his reservations sending me to Norman to learn milking.

'You'll have to learn it,' he said, 'but it does rather upset the routine, and cows hate their routine upset. You can go for a week with Norman, but keep out of the way as much as possible. Norman and Henry are wonderful cowmen, but they do like to get on in their own manner.'

I took the hint that they disliked their routine upset as much as the cows, and endeavoured to keep in the background, but when one of the cows urinated copiously into Norman's Wellington boot on my first day, it hardly augered well for the rest of the week.

'They doesn't like strangers,' he said with ill-concealed fury, 'That's why she done it.'

I lasted precisely two days in Norman's dairy, carrying out the menial chores of hosing down, opening bags of feed and cleaning the yard – 'there's twice as much more dung there than usual,' Norman persisted, hammering the message home, 'they knows something's up,' – and during milking I was advised to stand well back and watch. I was allowed, once and once only, to place the cluster on an old cow that was nearly dry, and this seemed to satisfy Norman that he had played his part in educating the next generation in the intricacies of milking.

I suspected Norman made strong representations to Mr. Chubb about the presence of a student in his dairy, and, to general relief all round, I was sent back to work on the land after two days, leaving Norman and Henry in peace with their herd of eighty mixed Guernsey and shorthorn cows, whose acquaintance I had hardly made. Those two days were the only experience of milking I had in eighteen months on Mr. Chubb's farm and dairying, not surprisingly, remained something of a mystery to me. Mr. Chubb was always evasive when I asked him when I was going to complete my week with Norman, and this incomplete week in the dairy became a standing joke on the farm.

''Ere, Davy, when's you going to finish off that week with Norm?' was a phrase that stayed with me until the end of my student days. But I never did. And it was probably just as well.

ᘓ

I thought I had become used to Mr. Chubb's wayward sense of humour, especially where it concerned his student, but when he announced at one of our weekly lunches that he was entering some of his cattle for the local show and I was to be in charge of them, I viewed the proposal with some scepticism. We had been drinking an extraordinarily powerful concoction of Mr. Chubb's before lunch, and he was in an expansive mood.

'We'll sweep the board and beat the lot of them,' he said, 'and you'll take as much credit as I will. It'll help you get started,' he said, leaning towards me and tapping me on the chest with his index finger, 'and that's what this game is all about – becoming known.'

I was doubtful, and after our lunch I mentioned Mr. Chubb's conversation to Fred. He pushed his cap back on his head and looked up at me.

'Same as I says, you, they lunches you 'as with Mr. Chubb ain't no good for neither of you. 'Ee does this every year, picks out three mad cattle an' expects us to 'ave 'em tame an' ready for the show in no time. It's a nightmare, I tells you. If youse two 'adn't 'ad them drinks 'ee might 'ave forgotten, an' 'ee don't mean you's in charge, 'ee means you's in charge of one animal. I knows 'ow 'is mind works, specially after dinner time.'

Fred's interpretation of Mr. Chubb's often misleading statements was always accurate – he had, after all, worked for him longer than anyone on the farm – and I was relieved I would not be 'in charge' of three highly strung, wild-eyed cattle on my own. I remembered treating them for warble flies all too clearly.

೧

Mr. Chubb enjoyed, as he put it, stirring the pot a little. 'It keeps people alert,' he told me, 'and sometimes produces surprising results.' He chose Fred to accompany Norman and myself to the show, and if Norman had any reservations, he kept them to himself. He needn't have worried, for the prospect of a day out at the show restrained Fred's jealousy of Norman's bonus and he was a model of co-operation, taking his orders without flinching.

Mr. Chubb had entered three animals, one shorthorn cow, one Guernsey cow and a shorthorn heifer. The two cows were not a problem, Norman had already selected them and started to prepare them; it was the heifer that was the difficulty. We went down to the water meadows where the heifers were peacefully grazing, and Mr. Chubb and James joined us there for the fraught process of finding the best of the bunch. It was rather like a meeting for everyone had his opinion, freely voiced, on the finer points of the heifers, and at one stage I thought we would be standing in the water meadows until the end of time. I was allowed no opinion – in any case I had little idea then what differentiated one heifer from another but suddenly Mr. Chubb turned to me. 'Which one would you have?' he asked.

I indicated one which appealed to me and he beamed.

'That's the very one I had in mind,' he said, and there was no further argument.

With considerable effort we separated her from her companions and drove her back to the dairy where we penned her prior to her three days intensive training for the show. She was not amused, which was hardly surprising as she had been happily unrestrained in a large field before she was so rudely interrupted and, remembering the wild streak in Mr. Chubb's shorthorns, I was doubtful we would be able to calm her in such a brief time, let alone get her used to a halter and grooming.

Mr. Chubb and James left us to make the preparations, with Norman in charge of Fred and myself.

'I'll take care of the cows,' he said to Fred. 'You and Davy can 'ave the 'eifer. If I gets any time, I'll give you an 'and, but I's got the milking too, mind. You'll 'ave to do the best you can.' Fred and I persevered, but it was not easy and at the cost of bruised shins and much bad language we managed to halter her, both of us determinedly pulling on the end of the halter and the heifer, equally determinedly pulling us towards her, rolling her eyes fiercely.

'You'll 'ave to do better than that,' said Norman, watching our amateur efforts. 'She's supposed to follow you along like a dog on a lead in a couple of days.'

It was after six o'clock when we left her reluctantly eating hay from a net, and bedded down comfortably in deep layers of straw. Fred, who lived in the next village, had missed his bus; Norman had smugly gone home and we were both exhausted.

'I could go a beer after that, Davy, while I waits for the bus.'

It seemed a good idea and after a couple of brown and milds Fred said, 'I 'opes you gets on alright with that 'eifer at the show.'

This was news to me. Thoroughly alarmed I said I thought as Fred and Norman had more experience, one of them should be in charge of the heifer and I should have one of the quieter cows.

'That heifer's never been brought into the dairy before,' I said, 'let alone carted off to a show.'

'Same as I says, Davy, me an' Norm reckons as you chose 'er, an' as you's younger than us, she's yourn. 'Sides, you's 'ere to learn an' that 'eifer'll learn you a thing or two.'

I slept uneasily that night.

∝

By the end of the second day we had her walking reluctantly round the yard on the end of the halter, and the day before the show Fred and I held her as firmly as we could while Norman expertly groomed her, and when he had finished even Fred was impressed.

'You'se done a good job there, Norm,' he said in a rare moment of praise. 'If Davy can keep 'is 'ead an' control 'er, we's in with a chance of winning.'

101

Mr. Chubb was even more optimistic. 'Best three cattle I have entered from this estate. They'll all bring back cups.'

' 'Ee says that every year,' said Norman after Mr. Chubb had gone home, 'An' 'ee's usually right. Don't you two be late in the morning, mind. The lorry's due at seven an' we'll need all the help we can get to load 'em.'

Despite Norman's doubts, the loading went without hitch, and the three of us squeezed uncomfortably into the cab with the driver for the short drive to the showground. I had never been to an agricultural show before, and I was surprised by the activity at such an early hour in the morning. As we bumped through the gateway the showground appeared chaotic; sheep were being driven to their pens, to the accompaniment of their shepherds' whistles and the barking of their dogs, cattle were noisily unloaded from their lorries, flowers and vegetables were tenderly lifted out from cars and carried to a cavernous tent, and on the trade stands the pristine agricultural machinery was having a final polish. It would probably be the last time it would receive such attention before, in working conditions, a quick blast with a high pressure hose to remove the worst of the mud would be the best treatment that could be expected. Horse boxes were arriving and discharging their cossetted loads, both two-legged and four-legged, and there was already a number of horses exercising around the showground.

We unloaded our cattle and my heifer showed signs of nervousness at the hubbub around her, but the two cows remained calm and this seemed, in turn, to calm her. Leaving Norman to carry out the finishing touches before the judging, Fred and I walked around the ground. The day was fine, which was just as well as it was only a one-day show, and I wondered at the effort that had gone into such organisation. For many, the local agricultural show was the social event of the year, and Fred was enjoying himself introducing me to his friends as 'Davy, my farm student', and giving me outrageous, unflattering potted histories of them afterwards. We passed the beer tent, already doing a good trade.

'We'll be in there for a while later,' Fred remarked. 'Norm, 'ee don't drink an' 'ee can look after the cattle.'

Mr. Chubb arrived with Mrs. Chubb. 'Best three animals the farm has produced,' he repeated to her. 'There will be prizes here.' And he was right; my heifer was first in her class, as was Fred's Guernsey, but Norman's shorthorn cow was show champion. Mr. Chubb was delighted; smiling broadly he gave Fred three pounds, 'to enjoy yourselves in the beer tent.'

''Ere,' said Fred magnanimously, 'you 'ave this pound, Norm, seein' you doesn't drink an' me an' Davy'll spend the rest in the beer tent. We'll need something before goin' in the ring with this lot.'

Startled, I asked Fred what he meant by 'goin' in the ring.' It sounded like a boxing match.

There was, he informed me, a grand parade of all the cattle in the afternoon, held in the showjumping ring. It was the highlight of the day, he explained, and with all the crowds around the ring, and all the strange cattle, he was worried how our three would behave.

'All they other cattle's used to it,' he said, 'they goes to all the shows. Ours, they's no idea. We's 'ad trouble before,' he added gloomily. We drank another beer and made our way back to prepare for the parade.

Norman was to lead the parade with Mr. Chubb's champion shorthorn cow. Fred was further back and I was near the end with the heifer class. There were crowds of people watching and I could feel the nervousness of my charge transmitting itself to me through the rope of the halter. The long line of cattle, each animal led by a stockman, slowly wound its way into the ring and as I entered I felt my heifer becoming increasingly restless, the noise from the crowd and the novelty of so many other cattle were unsettling her. It was a far cry from her lush water meadows where only a few days earlier she had been leading such an ordered life, and it was hardly surprising she should react to this alien atmosphere. The jumps had been left in position

for the parade, and as we passed close by one she leant heavily against me, relentlessly pushing me into it. Frantically trying to push her off and hold on to the halter at the same time, I was forced to try and climb over the wooden poles.

The crowd loved it and cheered lustily, but the sudden collapse of the jump, with the poles and uprights noisily tumbling to the ground and the roars of accompanying laughter proved too much for my prizewinning heifer; she took off with the speed of a greyhound, resolutely overtaking the other animals whilst I desperately kept hold of the halter, running faster than I had ever run before. As we roared past an unsuspecting Fred and his Guernsey, she recognised us and pulled Fred out of the line, following us at the same break-neck speed, Fred unsuccessfully endeavouring to control the expletives that came to him so readily in times of crisis. We came to the head of the procession, led by Norman and Mr. Chubb's champion cow, and they, too, in a manner quite disregarding the dignity expected of a head cowman and champion cow, gave chase. We circled the ring to the accompaniment of laughter, clapping and unmentionable comments from some sections of the crowd, undoubtedly fuelled by a long session in the beer tent. Their faces passed in a catherine-wheel blur, and still led by my out of control heifer and myself, tore through the exit from the ring. We raced through the showground, scattering astonished showgoers in our wake, and eventually came to a halt by a fence in the lorry park, so out of breath we could scarcely speak. I dreaded the thought of my next young farmers meeting.

All the rebellion had gone from our cattle, and we slowly led them back to their pen, tying them to the rail. Norman sat on an upturned bucket and lit a cigarette. Fred and I returned to the beer tent.

'Same as I says, you,' said Fred, wiping the froth from his mouth with the back of his hand after a long draught from his pint, 'next time we does a show I'll get some of they trannillisers from the chemist an' mix 'em in the feed before we starts. I couldn't go through that again.'

Neither could I, and there were still the young farmers to face.

Ꮻ

The corn was ripening fast, even to my inexperienced eye. 'Another three weeks or so, depending on the weather, and we'll be combining,' Mr. Chubb told me.

For me those three weeks, extended to four by a brief wet spell, were the halcyon days of summer. There was a relaxed atmosphere on the farm before the onset of harvest, the most important single event in the farming year, and although we were still working from seven o'clock to five o'clock, there was the thought in the back of the mind that soon we would be working hours far in excess of these. All the farmworkers took advantage of this comparative lull in activity to arrive home at a reasonable time, have their tea and tend their gardens in the evenings, knowing full well there would be little time for this in the ensuing weeks.

I went to London one Friday evening to a summer ball. I borrowed the Morris Minor from my long suffering mother and drove the old car the sixty-odd miles there. It was a superb ball, in aid of a worthy charity, with breakfast included in the price of the ticket.

To my amusement, I was treated with patronising sympathy by my friends and acquaintances – 'He's learning farming, you know.' If only they did know. The false ideal of town life, with its bright lights, its frenetic and artificial atmosphere was fast fading from my mind.

I left the great smoky city at five o' clock in the morning, and driving along the main road that wound through the farm, I reflected that only Norman and Henry would be at work milking their cows, and some of the early risers were probably drinking their first cups of tea of the day, lighting their first cigarettes or pipes and wandering leisurely up their gardens admiring their vegetables and flowers before ambling over to the farmyard to receive their orders for the day.

I parked the car as quietly as I could, carefully hung up my dinner jacket and changed into my farm clothes. As I had already breakfasted at a ridiculously early hour, I made myself a cup of tea and slowly drank it, reading the previous day's newspaper. At least my father could not complain I had burnt the fat for my fried breakfast that morning.

Mr. Chubb was on a fortnight's golfing holiday in Scotland, and James was left in charge of the farm. We had been clearing out the corn stores in the old farrowing sheds and he instructed me to take 'my' Ferguson and up there to help. The events of the previous night, the ball and the long drive were at last catching up with me, and I yawned deeply.

'What's the matter with you?' James asked. 'Have you been up all night?'

' 'Ee's been gallyvantin' with 'is town friends,' Wilf answered for me.

' 'Ee won't be no good for nothing this morning.'

James gave me a penetrating stare. 'You had best get up to the sheds before you fall asleep.'

It is often said that dreams are fleeting, lasting only micro-seconds and quickly forgotten. I can vouch for the former, but not the latter. I was captain of the *Queen Mary* navigating her through thick fog on the approach to Southampton Water. The fog horn was blaring monotonously, at first intermittently, then continuously. Something was wrong, and I suddenly jerked awake. The Ferguson was in the middle of the narrow lane and, horn blaring, pulled over into the bank as far as possible was the Old Man's shiny Daimler with Ron his chauffeur sitting white-faced at the wheel. It was fortunate for me he was on his way to collect his employer from the station and not the other way round, but he left me in no doubt about his views of farm students, 'Playin' around at farming and living it up at the same time.'

'You wants to get to bed of a night time, nipper, you won't learn nothing if you's asleep all the time,' he said.

He huffily resumed his seat in the Daimler and drove off to collect the Old Man without giving me another glance. His daughter was an avid member of the young farmers' club and, wide awake now, I continued my journey to the farrowing sheds, gloomily reflecting that after the débâcle of the show, and now this, I would somehow have to redeem myself.

'The Old Man wouldn't 'ave minded if you'd 'it 'is Daimler,' Fred informed me later. ''Ee's got a sense of 'umour and plentys of money, but Ron would 'ave killed you. 'Ee loves that car more than 'is missus.'

It was not the only time I fell asleep on a tractor.

∞

We were preparing for the farm competition in Mr. Chubb's absence. These competitions were held annually, the various farms categorised by acreage, but an outright winner could come from any class. Sam, a slight man in his late fifties with only one lung, spent his days before the competition behind an Allen Scythe, a monstrous grass-cutting machine with two large wheels, a reciprocating blade and powered by a temperamental Villiers two-stroke engine. The bare metal handles vibrated rhythmically in sympathy with the blades, and I found after about half-an-hour using one of these machines my hands shook as though I had a form of palsy. 'We calls 'em man eaters,' Sam told me, and I didn't disagree with him. When I saw him shaking his way along the verges in charge of his 'man eater', the long grass and tall nettles falling, clouds of blue smoke coming from the exhaust and blowing in his face (he always believed in adding more oil rather than less to the mixture) I wondered how such a small thin man could survive a man-eater, but Sam possessed a wiry strength and, despite his single lung, seemed to thrive on it. It was difficult to imagine the portly and excitable Wilf carrying out the same job with such equanimity, but Mr. Chubb knew which jobs to allocate his men.

He took the competition seriously and the farm had won it outright on several occasions. There were no half measures with Mr. Chubb and, James told me, he had left strict instructions for the estate to be immaculate and ready for the judges on his return from holiday.

Rounding the corner by the workshop one morning my way was blocked by Sam's tractor and trailer, with the Allen Scythe loaded up. It made frequent excursions to the workshop for repair, and Sam and Cecil, the full-time mechanic, had run it up a couple of planks onto the trailer, disappearing into the dark depths of Cecil's cavernous and greasy kingdom for a chat and a cup of tea. Jumping onto Sam's tractor, I started it up and was moving off when I heard a shout. Sam, alerted by the sound of his tractor, was standing by the high sliding doors of the workshop, the cup of tea held in his unsteady hand slopping its contents on the ground. He pointed at the trailer and I looked behind. The Allen Scythe had not been roped, and was rapidly moving down the trailer towards the open end. I slammed on the brakes and it came charging back, hitting the headboard with such force that it rebounded and once again, like a machine determined to self destruct, continued its inevitable progress down the bed of the trailer. I tried desperately to snatch the gear lever into reverse, but it was hopeless and the Allen Scythe inverted itself with a resounding crash onto the concrete.

It was a sorry sight, the wheels slowly rotating – one clockwise, the other anti-clockwise, the fuel tank flattened over the engine and petrol steadily running down the slope.

'You done it now,' said Cecil, slowly shaking his head, 'you really done it now.'

Not surprisingly James was furious, and I took my dressing-down as best I could, only explaining I had not wrecked the Allen Scythe on purpose. He refused to speak to me in the mornings, issuing my orders via someone else.

'Don't you worry, Davy boy,' Fred said when I mentioned I thought James's attitude was rather extreme. 'I's seen 'im 'ave these turns before an' 'ee soon gets over 'em.'

The fact that he did possibly owed something to an unfortunate experience he had on his own account with another Allen Scythe a few days later. These machines operated with a dog clutch, like the elevators, and the dog clutch was notoriously difficult to disengage at times. He took the handles of Sam's scythe for a short time and, unable to stop it, went up a bank into a field of barley where he cut a swath some thirty yards long before bringing the machine to a halt.

'They things 'as got minds all of their own,' said Sam with a smile.

We came second in the competition, and Mr. Chubb was content. The small matter of one ruined Allen Scythe was never mentioned again.

સ

8.

Clearing the Rats:
Preparation for Harvest

The Simms family had arrived from a farm in Sussex to work for Mr. Chubb some eighteen months before. Apart from myself and the natural progression of farmworkers' sons leaving school and coming to work on the land, the Simms were the first new blood Mr. Chubb had employed for over twenty years. 'Old Man Simms' as he was known by everyone except Fred, who more accurately called him 'Old Crafty', belonged to that wiry breed of farmworkers, like Sam, who were to be found on so many farms in the early 1960's. His two sons, Ray and Geoff, aged about thirty-five and forty respectively, also worked full-time on the farm. Old Man Simms was a bright, cocky man who thought the sole purpose of a student was to run errands for him, and he reacted angrily when he found this was not the case. Ray was a sullen man with staring pale blue eyes who seldom spoke, preferring to leave that chore to his loquacious father. He was of similar stature and, if gossip was to be believed, of a similar devious disposition. They were not liked by the other farmworkers – or the student, come to that – but Old Man Simms was made of stern stuff and didn't let that bother him. After all, he had had over sixty years experience to adjust to his colleagues disliking him and he took it in his stride. Ray's reaction was more difficult to fathom as he was so sparing of speech, and I suspected in his introspective withdrawn mind he harboured a deep resentment. Like his brother, Geoff, he was unmarried.

Geoff was different altogether – a large, strong, cheerful man, well liked by everyone and a complete contrast to his father and brother. 'There's bin a different ram in there,' Fred once told me mysteriously. They lived in a cottage opposite the sheep dip, almost as remote as Pal's, and Old Man Simms's wife could sometimes be seen walking down the lane to the shop – a short dumpy woman, with long, grey, unkempt hair and bulging varicose veins, a faded, downtrodden woman worn out by years of unappreciated caring for her family.

Geoff often helped Fred in both the feed mill and the dryer, and I was in the dryer when Fred suddenly said, 'Show Davy your trick, Geoff.' He found a length of binder twine, rapidly looped it around the lifting bar in the centre of a fifty-six pound weight, tied it off, and, placing the twine in his mouth, lifted the half hundredweight lump of metal from the floor.

'I ain't never seen that done afore,' said Fred. 'That's something to tell your young farmers.'

They were an unlikely pair, Fred and Geoff, but they had a certain rapport. Underneath Fred's rough and ready exterior there was a kindly man, and I think he felt sorry for Geoff and admired his cheerfulness.

'You got ter admire 'im, living with that 'orrible old man and brother an' that dirty ugly old woman, yet 'ee's always cheerful.'

That ' 'orrible old man' as Fred so succinctly described him, had originally been taken on as a manual worker, but when tractors became spare because of holidays or sickness he, like Pal, often drove one of the Fordsons for a while. He had a unique style of driving these tractors, definitely not a way the manufacturer would have recommended. When he pressed the starting lever and the engine fired, he carefully set the throttle to about three-quarters speed, or slightly more, and there it remained all day. Any subsequent adjustment of speed was effected by copious slipping of the clutch or, sometimes, a reluctant change of gear. At lunchtimes he came into the yard, half out of control, the tractor bouncing over the uneven surface, engine roaring, his feet alternately working brake and clutch, manoeuvred into position and, to general relief, stopped the engine. Not surprisingly he wore out expensive clutches in no time at all and Mr. Chubb stopped him from tractor driving. He professed an interest in gardening, and he was banished to work in the gardens, from where he was occasionally recalled to the farm when we were shorthanded.

ⴂ

We enjoyed a spectacularly hot week's pre-harvest weather which plunged Mr. Chubb into the depths of gloom. ('It can't last like this for much longer. It will end in thunder and flatten the corn.') Half the farm was on holiday and Old Man Simms was taken away from his gardening and sent with me to horse-hoe some beans. 'Horse-hoeing' was a carry over from the days when one man sat astride a metal seat on a wheeled hoe, the horse slowly plodding down the lines, the man steering the hoe, which took in about seven lines, by means of a curved bar set in front of him. The job required concentration, for one false move by horse or man and seven rows of the crop were neatly hoed out. The 1960's version was very little different from the original horse-drawn model; only the horse had changed.

'Don't you go too fast, mind,' Old Man Simms said. 'I ain't done this for a while an' it takes a time to get back into it again.'

He had no fear: I had never done it before and did not intend to break any records.

The field was some seven acres, completely flat and enclosed by hedges. It was one of the hottest days of the year, and for the first few passes I concentrated furiously on keeping the tractor on the correct line and driving straight to minimise the corrections from the hoe behind. I soon got the hang of it, and we crawled up and down the field, hour after hour, pausing only for the odd tea break. The day was becoming hotter and hotter, and after lunch the humidity was almost intolerable. A combination of the heat, a glass of beer at lunchtime and the snail's pace of the horse-hoeing contrived to make me very sleepy indeed and, although I made every effort to keep awake, I succumbed and my eyes closed. It was probably the shadow from the hedge that woke me. I stopped, horrified, and looked behind me. Old Man Simms was slumped across the steering bar, fast asleep, and he hadn't hoed out a single bean.

'Same as I says, you wants to watch this goin' to sleep on tractors, Davy,' said Fred. 'You mightn't be so lucky next time.'

ଔ

My father was secretary to the local flower show. This was no ordinary flower show held in a village hall, but a huge event encompassing the whole valley and outlying villages from miles around. In size and popularity it almost rivalled the agricultural show and for the young there was the added attraction of a travelling funfair which continued far into the night. It was a busy time for my father, organising the hire of the marquees, ensuring the funfair had the correct date and mediating in the many disputes, both minor and major that were inevitable in such a large undertaking. Most onerous was the paperwork, and I used to help him in the evenings, in return for a couple of bottles of beer, sorting out the entries and stamping the cards which were issued to each exhibitor. It was tedious, undemanding work, writing the name and class from the entry form onto a card, and stamping it. The name Simms cropped up with monotonous regularity, with entries for nearly every flower and vegetable class, and I idly wondered if it was Old Man Simms.

'He must have a large garden if it is him,' my father remarked, and indeed most of the farmworkers' gardens were of generous proportions. On the morning of the show the 'Simms' on the entry form proved none other than our own Old Man Simms, fussing about with his entries, ordering Ray and Geoff to unload them from the small trailer towed behind his flashy car which he drove with the same verve as he drove a tractor. He did not believe in working when there were others to do the work for him, and satisfied his 'boys' knew what they were doing he went to the beer tent. I complimented him on the quality of his produce.

'There's a tidy few prizes waiting there, boy,' he said, turning back to his drink in what I took to be a rare show of modesty, and he was right, for he won prize after prize. The cash involved must have been considerable for the flower show committee was generous in its reward for what it considered honest endeavour, but something bothered me about Old Man Simms.

There was little contact between the farmworkers and the gardeners but I remembered Gordon, the head gardener, had been in hospital for several weeks and his deputy had departed for another job, leaving Old Man Simms and a simple-minded youth in charge. The old man himself was enjoying one of his many cruises, and it would have been easy for him to have entered the best produce in his own name. I returned to the marquee and took another look at the exhibits. He hadn't been very subtle, for in nearly every case his employer's entries were second or third and the best the gardens could provide were surrounded by first prize certificates under the name of 'Simms'.

It was generally reckoned on the farm that he had bought everything he entered from the market: no one seemed to make the connection, and with harvest on the horizon, no one cared very much. I remained quiet, thinking the old boy would probably overstep the mark sooner or later.

ଓ

I was clearing some rubbish from the dryer, wheeling the sacks onto the trailer which was backed up tight to the loading ramp, when Mr. Chubb's Land Rover rounded the corner and slowly climbed the steep hill. He stopped, switched off the engine and climbed out, leaving it rocking on the hill in gear, the handbrake off. He studied it for a moment.

'Why's that thing rocking?' He asked me.

'I expect you forgot to put the handbrake on, Mr. Chubb,' I replied.

He grunted, opened the door and pulled it on.

Mr. Chubb liked to shock – I was becoming used to that now – but he also liked to ask for, and expected to receive, honest opinions from his student. He enjoyed putting me on the spot by asking for my views on a variety of subjects, most of which I knew very little about. It was partly his sense of humour and partly his way of keeping me on my toes ('you'll learn more than farming here', he had once told me with unintended irony). But when he suddenly said 'What do you think of Ray?' I was unprepared. I nervously glanced round to the open door of the dryer where Ray was helping Fred, and cleared my throat. But Mr. Chubb's question was rhetorical.

'He's useless,' he continued. 'I have never liked him, he gives me the creeps.' He leant towards me, his hands clasped together over his stick.

'Have you ever noticed those pale blue, staring eyes of his? I wake up in the night thinking about those eyes. There's bad blood in that boy.'

It was difficult to imagine such a forceful character as Mr. Chubb losing sleep over the pale blue staring eyes of one of his employees, but I knew there was more to come.

'I am going to sack him. I have never sacked anyone on this farm before but I am going to sack that boy.' (I thought this was rich coming from Mr. Chubb; it was a comment Jack would have relished) Most of my men have been with me for years, and that must mean something. That Simms family has never fitted in and they are best out of it. I'm going to sack him now and I'll sack his father later.'

He stalked off into the dryer and I continued loading my trailer. Ten minutes later he emerged, told me briefly to make sure I tipped my rubbish as far back in the dell as I could, and drove off. I couldn't believe he had sacked Ray in this short time, and when he was out of sight I went through

112

the door to find out what had happened.

' 'Ee's sacked Ray,' said Fred with satisfaction. Ray was sitting morosely on an upturned bucket, chewing a length of straw. He looked up at me with those pale eyes.

'I doesn't know what to do now,' he said. 'I ain't never 'ad the sack before.'

I found that difficult to believe too.

�☙

Old Man Simms virtually sacked himself. The Major had been doing the accounts for the gardens, and had noticed the large Dennis mower had been using a phenomenal amount of petrol. Suspecting Old Man Simms had been running his car on the mower account, he went over to the gardens to confront him. The old man vigorously denied the Major's allegations, and a furious row ensued, culminating in the Major informing Old Man Simms he would see Mr. Chubb that evening.

We never saw the Simms family again. The next morning they had gone, the house empty, their rubbish dumped in the garden and their bills unpaid. Where they went no-one ever knew – probably back to Sussex Fred reckoned – but their passing hardly caused a ripple in the well ordered life of the farm.

ᚲ

All activities were now centred on preparations for the harvest.

'It's the preparation that is so important,' Mr. Chubb impressed upon me, swirling the ice in the bottom of his glass before we went in to eat one of Mrs. Chubb's delectable lunches. 'If you have prepared thoroughly you cannot blame yourself for any disasters that might happen later, and there's always disasters at harvest.'

ᚲ

The most obvious sign of this 'pre-harvest panic', as Wilf put it, was the removal, one by one, of the three huge red Massey Ferguson 780 combine harvesters from their shed to Cecil's workshop which, large though it was, could only accommodate one of these machines at a time. Resembling enormous boiled crustaceans, Cecil crawled over and into these recumbent monsters like a tiny parasite, wielding his spanners and screwdrivers with authority as he poked at their vital parts.

The workshop was a gloomy, badly lit building, and Cecil used a lamp with a trailed lead to illuminate his incursions inside the combine; entering his workshop and seeing a combine dimly lit from within, with Cecil grunting and scraping around unseen in its innards, was an eerie experience: it was almost as if the combine was animated as in a children's cartoon. But the sight of Cecil, clad as ever in his greasy overalls emerging red-faced, covered in last year's straw and dust quickly dispelled the illusion.

I never saw Cecil wearing anything other than his greasy overalls – for all I knew they were the same unwashed ones he wore at the end of my eighteen months stint as a student as he had on when I started. They certainly looked the same, and he even wore them to the pub in the evenings to the glowering and sometimes vociferous disapproval of the landlady. Cecil was unmoved by her pointed comments, placidly sipping his pint, sitting in his chair by the fire.

He was a handsome man, in a biblical manner, with a hooked nose, hooded brown eyes and wavy black hair which, from his habit of constantly running his hands through it, was almost as greasy as his overalls. He lived like a hermit in his workshop, leaving it reluctantly to attend a breakdown, blinking in the unaccustomed daylight. I never thought of Cecil as having a home and I almost came to believe he spent most of his life in his dimly lit workshop. He was always there when I arrived in the mornings and it was easy to imagine he returned there to sleep when he was thrown out of the pub.

His workshop fascinated me. It had probably not been tidied up in the preceding forty-odd years, and it was stacked with spare parts for obsolete machines from another era, forming alleyways stretching far back into the seldom trodden and almost forgotten depths of the building. Cumbersome iron wheels vied for space with obscurely shaped cast-iron cogs and sprockets, mostly brand new, from some machine that had caught Mr. Chubb's fancy years ago and which was probably now lying rusting at the bottom of one of the many dells on the farm which we used as rubbish tips.

Mr. Chubb thought the world of Cecil, and had bought him an old Ford Thames van that, even by 1960's standards, was archaic. The driver's seat had lost most of its springs and was supported with blocks of wood and Cecil, not the tallest of men, could barely see over the steering wheel as he bounced across fields in his van to repair some stricken machinery. He also used this van to bounce to and fro from the pub, the passenger seat usually occupied by Wilf. The van was known throughout the farm and the village as 'The Pig'. Its number plate was appropriately prefixed by the letters SOW.

Cecil loathed Americans. He had fought, and, if he were to be believed, single-handedly won the battle of Monte Cassino and the experience had left him with a supreme contempt for our New World allies. He never lost an opportunity to vent his feelings on me regarding the Americans, maintaining Eisenhower had prolonged the war for many months: it was a familiar argument and probably correct. While he talked he laboriously rolled a cigarette, the grease from his fingers rendering the paper almost black, and I watched with interest as he lit these revolting smokes, wondering if they would ignite in a sheet of flame. They never did, but the grease must have imbued the cigarette with an interesting flavour.

Cecil had been a lance corporal in the army, and coincidentally several years later I worked on a sheep station in New Zealand where the owner, as a sergeant, had also won the battle of Monte Cassino. His views on the Americans were broadly similar to Cecil's, though more crudely stated, and I often wondered if the gentle mechanic from southern Hampshire had met the bigoted sheep farmer from New Zealand all those miles from their homes in a war-torn world neither of them knew or understood at all.

In the early 1960's there was little of the rush and tear that is associated with modern living, for it was a transitional time, a time when farms were undeniably overmanned and a time when the development of reliable farm machinery had yet to be attained. The tractor, with its innovative hydraulics, was scarcely different in principal from the modern tractor and just as dependable, but many of the implements it trailed behind were in their infancy of development and some hardly managed a pass down the field without a breakdown. Cecil was undoubtedly kept busy at seasonal times, driving out in the pig, rapidly effecting a repair and returning to his monastic existence in his workshop, but it was difficult to imagine how he occupied his time while he waited for these breakdowns to occur.

In the summer when I went into his workshop he would suddenly appear from nowhere, seemingly pleased to see someone, and regale me with long stories of his past: in the winter he was invariably sitting in front of an old coke burning stove drinking endless cups of tea. Sometimes I found him standing over a vice, slowly filing some piece of machinery and at other times he had his head buried under the bonnet of one of the Land Rovers. He was a completely happy man.

There was, however, a balance to be struck. Mechanisation was waiting in the wings, waiting to destroy a pattern of life that had continued for centuries and, indeed, on many farms it had already succeeded in destroying it, but the Old Man and Mr. Chubb were content to preserve the old order for a little while longer with a compassion and humanity seldom found in the modern world. Mr. Chubb ran the farm efficiently and profitably for the Old Man with none of the greed that would come later in the pursuit of greater efficiency, lower costs and, of course, less labour. For the moment machinery was working alongside the existing labour force in some harmony, but the machines were waiting to pounce, and it was a paradox that Cecil, one of the old brigade, was unknowingly in charge of the means of its destruction.

'He's a marvellous mechanic,' said Mr. Chubb, watching Cecil climbing around a combine. 'He really comes into his own at harvest.'

03

'You had best go and help Fred and Luke clear the drier down,' Mr. Chubb informed me one morning. 'It's a dusty job, but I always like the dryer cleared right down before we start harvest.'

Fred was in charge of the dryer.

'Same as I says, you, 'ee always leaves it till the last minute,' he grumbled as we trudged up the hill. 'If 'ee let me 'ave 'elp sooner we wouldn't 'ave this last minute panic. Same every year, mind, 'ee never learns.'

The dryer was a huge structure, clad in asbestos sheeting with a large building joined onto it containing six storage silos which were about sixty-five feet high. They had iron rings set in the concrete for access to the top, but a more modern addition was a narrow catwalk running along the tops of the silos reached by vertical iron ladders from the main dryer. These ladders also afforded entry to the uppermost workings of the dryer. Endless belts with metal cups, enclosed in wooden boxing, transported the grain up to the silos. The powerful oil-fired drying unit was housed in a separate part of the building. It seemed a complicated place, with control panels, chutes, belts, little glass spyholes in the wooden boxing, electric motors, hoppers and scales, but Fred had worked the dryer for years and knew its every intricacy. He saw me eyeing the vertical iron ladders.

'We 'ad land girls 'ere in the war,' he said, 'an' we sent they what wore skirts up the ladders in front of us. Ladies first, we said. We was real toffs then.'

He grinned toothlessly at me, savouring the memory.

' 'Ere, get on the end o' that brush an' sweep the floor. When you's finished, clear all them loose sacks up.'

I did as I was told, and the dust flew from the end of the wide broom like a thick grey fog, almost choking us. Fred opened the doors and the dust boiled out of the dryer as though it was on fire. There were layers of the stuff and soon Fred and I were covered in it, our clothes coated grey, our eyes streaming. When I had finished I started sorting out the pile of sacks carelessly discarded in the corner, neatly folding the sound ones into one heap and the ones with holes into another. I soon discovered these sacks were home to innumerable rats, and lifting the damp fusty sacks revealed nests writhing with naked pink baby rats which I flicked onto the floor and swept dispassionately out of the door.

'I 'ates them bloody things,' said Fred. 'Where you's got corn you's got rats an' you'll never be rid of 'im. My cats does their best but there's too many for 'em. We puts down poison all the time, but they rats always wins in the end.'

We heard a faint cry from Luke who had been sent on some errand along the catwalk which ran between the silos.

'What's 'ee want?' Asked Fred. 'I hopes 'ee ain't fallen in one of them silos – 'ee'll drown in the corn. We'd best whip up there quick.'

We climbed the ladders and hauled ourselves onto the catwalk running between the two banks of three silos, high in the roof of the dryer. In the dim light provided by two naked bulbs hanging from long flexes we saw Luke, his arms spread wide over a sack which was wrapped round a roof girder to protect incautious heads from contact with the unforgiving iron.

'Got a rat in there – a big 'un. Get a stick, quick, I can't 'old on much longer.'

I looked more closely and saw the sack was writhing and bulging as the captive rodent endeavoured to escape, but Luke had blocked its exits with his hands.

' 'Ee ran up the inside of the girder an' I waited 'till 'ee were in the sack an' pounced,' said Luke with satisfaction. 'You got that stick Fred?'

Fred despatched the rat with several heavy blows, and Luke let go of the sack. Luke had no fear of rats and I once saw him catch one by the tail, swing it in a semi-circle and crash its head onto the concrete.

'I don't know 'ow 'ee does it,' said Fred with distaste. 'I cain't bring myself to touch they bloody things.'

Fred sent Luke and I into one of the giant silos to clear some damp and fusty grain from the floor. It was a terrible job. We struggled through a small metal access hatch at the base – no easy task for Luke in his unyielding corsets – and fighting for purchase on the steeply sloping floor which funnelled the grain to a conveyor underneath, we shovelled the grain into bags which we laboriously thrust out of the hatch. Soon a green choking mould rose up from the corn, so thick it was difficult to see each other and, coughing and spluttering, we climbed through the hatch for some fresh air.

'See them dead rats in there?' asked Luke. 'If they cain't stick it down that 'ole there ain't much 'ope for me an' you.'

We persevered, working in short bursts, and just as we were finishing James and Fred peered through the hatch. It must have been an astonishing spectacle – Luke and I almost invisible in the swirling cloud of green mould and dust, wheezing and gasping like the alcoholic Admiral at the guest house as we filled the last sack.

'Come out of there at once,' James shouted. 'That mould will kill you.'

As we emerged, Luke creaking loudly as he struggled once again through the small opening, James turned to Fred angrily.

'Why didn't you give them face masks?' he asked him.

'You knows we never uses they things,' Fred replied. ' 'Sides, Davy's got to learn to do the job proper, that's what 'ee's 'ere for,' he added without guile.

'He won't be for much longer and neither will Luke if you make them work in conditions like that,' he said.

Fred was unrepentant. 'I's worked in worse than that,' he said, 'an' it ain't 'urt me.'

I turned to Luke, his crinkled face tinged green as though he was about to be horribly ill.

'Some says good old Fred, others speaks the truth,' he said with some feeling.

My mother looked askance at me when I came home for my lunch. 'I thought farming was supposed to be a healthy life,' she said when I told her what I had been doing. So did I, but at the time I felt I was suffering from the effects of a lifetimes heavy smoking.

愉

I spent three more days in the dryer with Fred and Luke, and in that time we bagged off about seventy tons of barley remaining in the silos from the previous year. There was no bulk corn on Mr. Chubb's farm; every grain that came in from the harvest field was dried, stored and despatched from the farm in thick hessian sacks, two hundredweights for barley and two-and-a-quarter hundredweights for the denser wheat which occupied the same space in the sack as the lighter barley. The end of the chain in the dryer was a large metal funnel sprouting from a platform high above like a huge ice cream cornet, and Fred expertly attached the sacks with a leather strap to the base of the cornet and weighed them off. The flow of the grain was controlled by a slide which Fred set with a precision gained by years of experience of the workings of the dryer.

'If she's open too wide there ain't no time to sew up the sacks an' wheel 'em away,' he said. 'Open 'er too little, the 'opper fills up an' the corn overflows all over yer 'ead.'

He sewed up the sacks using a large sack needle with an easy skill, leaving two neat ears at either end, and wheeled them away on his sack trucks into the loading bay where they leant against each other in regimented rows awaiting collection by the corn merchants' lorries.

'You'll 'ave to do better than that, Davy,' he said, critically surveying my first attempt to sew up a sack. 'It's got to be tight an' neat, an' they ears 'as to be even. Them lorry drivers'll curse you when they gets the like of that on their backs, kinking in the middle an' rattling corn around their ears. It turns the bed of the lorry into a skating rink with all the spilt corn, an' that ain't no joke when you's carrying a weight like that.'

I saw exactly what he meant the following day when the first lorry arrived and backed up the steep slope to the loading ramp belching clouds of sweet-smelling diesel smoke. The driver assembled a curious contraption resembling a cradle with a taut two-inch canvas strap running across it. This contraption was laid horizontally to the ramp, and I watched with interest as Fred wheeled the first sack of corn down to it on his sack trucks. The driver was standing in position, glancing over his shoulder, and Fred, stopping his sack trucks, tipped the bag of corn onto the cradle. The sack fell forward and hit the canvas strap which activated a hydraulic ram and the cradle rose up, describing a quivering arc with its immense load, neatly depositing it onto the shoulders of the waiting driver. Propelled by two hundredweight of barley held high on his back, he shot down the bed of the lorry, turned, dumped it by the headboard, and returned for the next sack.

Fred knew all the lorry drivers and some, for reasons of his own, he did not like. He exacted a particular revenge on these by tipping the sack on the cradle as the unfortunate man was still off-loading the previous one, waiting a second or two, and shouting, 'One on the way'. The driver, when he turned round, was confronted by a sack jerking high on the cradle and, sprinting up the lorry, roundly cursing Fred, turned to receive it on his back. We loaded lorries in record time in this way, but the cradle was a dreadfully dangerous device, requiring courage and split-second timing from the driver if he were not to injure his back. It had the advantage, from our point of view, that the sacks could be topped straight off the shoulder. With the lorries not equipped with the hydraulic cradle – and they were the majority – we had to top the heavy sacks from the bed where we tipped them: it was arduous work. I particularly remember an ancient six-wheeled Ford lorry which made the long trek up from South Devon. Its number plate, starting with the letters FHW said it all.

We soon cleared all the corn from the dryer, and Mr. Chubb moved us up to the old farrowing sheds.

ೞ

The Old Man had made his money from pigs, and at one stage the farm had been the largest pig farm in the south of England, but the advent of phosphates had made it economical to grow corn on the thin downland soil, and gradually corn replaced the pigs. The considerable profit from the corn enabled him to enter the industrial world and he prospered, leaving Mr. Chubb a free hand to run the estate.

The redundant farrowing sheds made ideal corn stores. Long, low, wide buildings, with doors large enough to allow a tractor and trailer to be driven inside, they were cool and weatherproof. They were not, however, rat-proof.

Several tons of bagged barley remained from the previous year's harvest, and Mr. Chubb had sold this cheaply to clear the shed for the new harvest. Our job was to load this onto trailers and take it back to the dryer to await collection – the farrowing sheds were too low to admit a lorry.

'You'd best find yourself a good stout stick, Davy,' said Wilf. 'We 'as a good rat 'unt up there when we clears the last of the corn.'

We took three tractors and trailers to the farrowing shed, and everyone who was spare climbed aboard the trailers armed with their sticks. There must have been ten of us altogether and, judging from the conversation, the rat hunt was an eagerly awaited highlight of the farming year.

When we pulled back the heavy doors, I looked inside, expecting the floor to be crawling with rats, but there were none. Disappointed and mystified, and suspecting another student leg pull, I scathingly asked Wilf where all his rats had gone.

'They's over there, nipper,' he said, indicating a neat stack of bagged corn halfway down the building. 'You keep 'old of your stick an' you'll soon see.'

We backed the first tractor and trailer to the stack and started loading, two to a sack, hands firmly clasped together, lifting the deadweight sacks of barley up onto the trailer. After we had loaded the second trailer, there was still no sign of the rats.

'Any time now, nipper,' said Wilf, his eyes gleaming with anticipation. One by one the rats declared themselves, fleeing the dwindling stack as we loaded the last trailer, squeaking with fear before being silenced for ever by a well aimed blow from a stick or a mighty kick from a steel capped toe of a hobnailed boot. Fred soon gave up the unequal task of stitching the holes they had gnawed and we cast the last remaining sacks to one side. There were rats everywhere now, running in all directions, vigorously pursued by farmworkers and a student who was rapidly becoming an expert at despatching rats.

'Look out, Jack,' shouted Fred, 'there's a bugger coming straight at yer.'

Jack was carefully rolling a cigarette, and a huge brown rat, bent on suicide or self preservation, was racing towards him.

' 'Ee'll go up yer trouser leg,' Fred yelled urgently. Jack continued rolling his cigarette, unmoved, ignoring the fast approaching rodent. We watched, enthralled. At the last moment Jack performed an act of instant levitation that would have done credit to a magician, and the rat ran under Jack's hobnails at the precise time they decided to return to the hard concrete.

He silently kicked the flattened rat to one side and continued rolling his cigarette. It was an impressive performance, and it was also the last rat.

CB

We drew the final load of corn up to the doors, swept the dead rats out of a side door and re-bagged the salvageable barley.

' 'Ere, Davy,' said Fred when we had finished, ' 'ow far does you reckon the end of the shed is from the back of the trailer?'

I eyed the distance. 'About fifty yards,' I replied.

'I bets you half-a-crown you cain't carry one of they sacks of barley off the back of the trailer to the end of the shed an' return without droppin' it,' he said.

I had never carried a full sack of corn on my back before, but there was more than an idle bet at stake here.

'I'll give it a try,' I said, 'for half-a-crown.'

Fred slapped my hand. 'Done,' he said with satisfaction. He faced the others. ' 'Ee'll never do it, 'ee'll never get 'alf way. That 'alf crown's as good as good as mine; it's a racing certainty.'

'And you'll be on your way if you crocks Mr. Chubb's student with your stupid bet,' said Jack. He turned to me. 'You ever carried a bag of corn before?' I told him I hadn't. 'It's your back you wants to take care of,' he said. 'If you feels the bag slipping on your shoulders, don't 'ang on to it, let it go – else you'll put your back out for the rest of your life. The higher you gets the bag on your shoulders, the easier it is. 'Ere, 'ave a trial run before you starts.'

I noticed that in spite of his admonishment to Fred he was as keen as the rest to see if I could complete the distance. He gently tipped a two hundredweight sack of barley onto my shoulders from the trailer and I tottered a few faltering steps around the shed. My legs felt like jelly, but providing I kept the sack high, with my arms extended, the weight didn't seem too bad. Nonetheless, two hundredweights was an awesome load, especially when related to the weight of a human. I tried to imagine carrying a fat sixteen-stone woman a hundred yards on my back, but abandoned the attempt.

'Sees what I means, Davy?' asked Fred. 'Does you want to call it off an' give me my half-crown now?'

There was no turning back, so I declined Fred's offer and positioned myself by the trailer ready for the off. Jack tipped the sack forwards, I took it and started. The first twenty yards were relatively easy, but after that I felt the sack slowly sliding down my back, becoming heavier and heavier, trying to pull me over with its weight. After thirty yards it was hopeless and I took Jack's advice and dropped it.

'Told you it were a racing certainty,' said Fred. 'You owes me 'alf a crown.'

But I knew where I had gone wrong; it was a matter of balance, and keeping the arms rigid and I was convinced I could do it, given a second attempt.

'Double or quits,' I said to Fred, knowing he wouldn't be able to refuse.

'If that's what you wants, Davy,' he said, 'but it's your funeral.'

Once again I set off, staggering slightly under the weight, but this time

122

I felt I had the measure of it and the balance right. I reached the end of the farrowing shed and turned round carefully: the trailer and my crowd of onlookers seemed an impossible distance away and my legs were beginning to feel like leaden weights that didn't belong to the rest of my body. This was my own one-horse race and I felt I had something to prove. I was determined to complete the course and collect my five shillings from Fred.

With ten yards left, I had my doubts. It was becoming increasingly difficult to place one foot in front of the other, my eyes were misted and stinging from the sweat pouring off my brow and my arms were shaking uncontrollably. I made an extra effort to spur myself on. Just as I thought I would never reach that blurred trailer surrounded by a knot of shouting and excited farmworkers, I heard Fred's voice above the others calling, 'Come on, Davy, you can make it'. And I did, just, twisting the sack off onto the floor and collapsing on top of it, exhausted. Fred thumped me on my tender back and said with unintended double irony, 'Well done Davy. The other Davy couldn't 'ave done that, 'ee never did like a bet.'

'Davy's 'ere to learn, but 'ee's learnt you something, Fred,' said Wilf. 'What's that?' asked Fred.

'There ain't no such thing as a racing certainty,' replied Wilf.

ભ

Wilf introduced me to the dubious and addictive delights of smoking. At one of our tea breaks he offered me his tin of tobacco, and it gave him great amusement watching me endeavour to roll a cigarette. When I lit my inexpertly rolled smoke, at the same time disappointing Wilf by not coughing as he had expected, I found I rather enjoyed it, and I soon became quite proficient at the art of hand rolling. Just as soon Wilf realised his joke had backfired on him and ceased proffering his tin at tea break time, so I resorted to buying my own tobacco. I could never come to terms with the cold tea the others drank in the summer months, but I happily puffed on my home-made roll ups as we sat around talking. I made sure Mr. Chubb – and my mother, for that matter – never discovered my new habit, hastily extinguishing my cigarette when I heard the familiar noise of an approaching Land Rover. This amused Wilf.

'You'd best behave yourself, nipper,' he said. 'If I tells Mr. Chubb you's taken to smoking, 'ee'll tell your folks an' then you'll be for it.'

This was true. I was more worried my parents should not find out their son had taken up smoking than I was if Mr. Chubb discovered my vice. A chance remark from him to my mother could cause difficulties.

'He still doesn't know how you broke your toe back in the spring,' I reminded him. Wilf grunted derisively. 'That's all in the past. 'Ee's got a short memory, an' 'ee won't worry 'imself about that no more.'

He grinned at me through his piratical beard, so dense I could barely see his teeth. 'So watch it, nipper, just watch it.'

I wasn't sure what it was I had to watch, but his words proved prophetic in a way Wilf had not intended.

ભ

Rain had delayed the start of the harvest, and I was trimming a field high on the downs, a plateau edged with stunted hawthorn hedging so gnarled and twisted it looked as if it had been fighting the unequal battle against the gales that swooped up the down from the beginning of time. I stopped the tractor and switched off the engine: it was time for a cigarette. As the monotonous roar of the tractor's engine slowly left my ears it was replaced by another sound – a far-off angry shouting drifting up to me on the breeze. It was rather like listening to the announcements broadcast from a fête in the next village on a calm summers day, muffled but discernable. Curious, I climbed off my tractor and peered through the battered hedge. A bizarre spectacle greeted me. Wilf, deputising for Alan, who had taken advantage of the wet weather to enjoy a couple of days holiday, was rounding up the sheep, and the round up was not going well. Wilf's tractor and trailer were parked by the yards and, standing on the trailer watching Wilf with interest, were three dogs – two of Alan's collies and a dog of indeterminate breed which belonged to Wilf. Wilf was trying to drive the sheep into a pen on his own without canine assistance. I could guess what had happened. He had lost his temper with the dogs, they had taken revenge and returned to the trailer, leaving him to get on with the round up on his own.

I settled down to enjoy the fun. Sheep were scattered all over the steeply sloping field, but Wilf was concentrating on a knot of about ten, presumably thinking they would form the nucleus of a mob that he could single-handedly drive into the yards. He hadn't a hope. Wilf, a heavily built man, had lost all control of his temper, his body and the sheep. He was tearing downhill, driven by his own momentum, roaring at the top of his voice every insult to sheep and The Almighty he could summon. He carried a crook in his right hand which he brandished alarmingly but ineffectively at the sheep, which easily outpaced him. From my high vantage point it seemed as if the sheep were teasing Wilf, pacing themselves to him, increasing their speed to his,

and slowing down when they thought he was too far behind. Suddenly, at full speed, arms flailing wildly, Wilf fell, tumbling end over end, his crook flying in the air. He lay still on the ground, and the sheep instantly stopped running and started contemptuously grazing, glad to be free from their tormentor. Wilf stirred, sat up and started rubbing his leg. Slowly he rose to his feet and retrieved the crook. With a mighty shout he whirled it round his head like a Highland hammer thrower and hurled it at the surprised sheep and, leaving it where it fell, limped painfully back to the tractor where his dogs, unimpressed, now lay asleep in the shade under the trailer.

The next morning Wilf limped into the farmyard.

'How did you hurt your leg, Wilf?' I asked him. He glared at me. 'Hurt me ankle jumping off the tractor, if you must know,' he replied.

'Nothing to do with rounding up sheep?' I enquired.

'Now look 'ere nipper,' he began.

'I was having a quiet smoke on top of the hill,' I went on, 'when I heard this noise.'

I offered him my tobacco tin. He took it and grinned.

'Alright, nipper,' he said. 'I takes the 'int. But you'd still better watch it or I'll 'ave yer.'

Two days later we started the corn harvest.

ଔ

9.

Harvest

❛ The corn harvest is the most important event in the year on this farm,'
Mr. Chubb had told me at our last weekly lunch before the great moment.
'The potatoes, the sugar beet, the hay – they are nothing. It's the corn that
makes the money here, the money that keeps the farm going. This is some
of the best corn-growing land in the country, and we grow the best corn
here, on this estate.' It was no idle boast: Mr. Chubb had few peers in the
corn growing stakes.

'The Old Man bought this farm for a pittance,' he continued, 'and went
in for pigs, but the advent of phosphates made it possible to grow corn on
the thin downland soil, and the farm became worth fifty times the amount
he paid for it, so he got rid of his pigs and turned the land to corn. He didn't
know much about growing corn, so he looked for a good manager, and that
is how I started working for him.' There was no false modesty to Mr. Chubb.
'I have worked more harvests than most people here.' He paused and pointed
his index finger at me. 'How old do you think I am?'

This was dangerous ground. It was not the first time he had asked me
the question and I had learnt his age varied according both to his mood and
the number of drinks he had consumed. I had also learned to keep quiet, for
the question was always rhetorical.

'I am nearly eighty,' he said with satisfaction, 'and I might make this
my last harvest and retire,'

'Charles says this every year,' Mrs. Chubb told me, 'but I don't think he
will ever retire.'

Mr. Chubb leant back in his chair, his hands clasped over his waistcoat,
smiling contentedly.

෧

We broke ourselves in gently to the harvest, starting on a fifteen-acre
field of oats, close to the river. The mist was slowly rising from the river,
waiting for the sun's rays to strengthen and overpower it, the tall oats swaying
slightly in the almost imperceptible breeze, waiting for the cutter bar and
the threshing drum.

The three giant red combine harvesters stood just inside the gateway waiting, like us, for the dew to evaporate so we could start to harvest eight hundred acres of grain in a month of hard and unrelenting work. I was also looking forward to supplementing my £1 a week wage with plenty of overtime, including working on Saturdays and Sundays. I needed the money.

Jack, Alan and Wilf were the combine drivers; Brian, Desmond and myself the corn carters. Desmond, Wilf's nephew, was a huge gangling young man of about twenty-four, as placid as Wilf was volatile, immensely strong but at the same time lacking a certain control over his powerful limbs. He had a curious nasal inflection to his voice which was easily imitated, and it was difficult, when speaking to him, not to reply in the same adenoidal tones. Cecil had parked the pig – now a mobile workshop, heavily weighed down with his tools – by the combines and was busy making last minute adjustments to the concaves and threshing drums. We stood by the trailers, fitted with their high corn sides, with sacks hanging on the insides of the swinging tailboards to plug the gaps, smoking and waiting for Mr. Chubb to give his starting orders. We saw the canvas top of his Land Rover as he drove down the lane and hastily extinguished our cigarettes – smoking was strictly forbidden in the highly combustible harvest fields – as he drove through the gateway. He and James inspected the oats and confirmed the result of our own inspection a quarter-of-an-hour earlier: we were ready to begin.

The combines started with grumbling roars and clouds of smoke; they pirouetted neatly into position, lowered their header tables and, in staggered formation, cut into the oats in a wide swath around the headland. Soon they became indistinct, the dust and the shimmering heat combining to fade their images, and the noise, too, faded into the distance, leaving a temporary peace. The only evidence of their presence was a muffled drumming and a far-off trail of dust.

James had ridden off on Jack's machine, standing on the steps watching the oats falling to the cutters and hypnotically augured into the opening to the threshing drum. Mr. Chubb had been talking to Cecil. He came over to us, leaving Cecil to sift through the straw left in the combines' wake, looking for evidence he had made his adjustments correctly and the oats were going into the combines' storage tanks rather than out of the back of the machines.

'Have you all got your sheets?' he enquired. Our canvas sheets were all neatly tied to the fronts of our trailers, and Mr. Chubb beamed. 'Never forget your sheets. You must have them with you all the time, and when you change trailers, don't forget to take the sheet with you.'

He went back to see how Cecil's procrastinations in the straw were progressing.

' 'Ee's got a thing about them sheets,' said Brian. 'Every time 'ee meets you in the lane 'ee always asks you two questions: 'ave you got your sheet an' 'ow many loads 'ave you done? It don't matter about the loads, you can tell 'im any number you likes an' 'ee'll be 'appy, but if you ain't got your sheet you'll be in big trouble. An' that's another thing. Never keep a combine waiting. If they 'as to stop because the tank's full, everyone goes mad – an' you know what Wilf's like – but it ain't easy when you's the only one in the field an' all three combines is nearly full. It's always us corn carters what gets the blame for stopping the 'arvest, and it ain't 'ardly ever our fault.'

Soon the combines reappeared and, in well rehearsed routine, separated and started marching across the field, each one purposefully cutting out its own section of oats. Emptying the corn from the combines presented no problems, driving alongside the machine in the same way as silage making. When the driver judged the tractor and trailer was in the correct position he pulled a lever and the auger and spout – attached to the side of the combine like a thick tentacle – burst into life with a quivering clatter and an inevitable cloud of dust. There was a slight delay as the grain worked its way up the auger, then it came pouring from the spout, falling to the bed of the trailer, spreading out from a mound to cover the floor. This was where the corn carter had to use skill, spreading the load evenly using clutch and throttle.

Unlike silaging, where a little spilt grass was of no consequence, a pile of corn lying on the ground in mute testimony of a momentary lapse in concentration was almost as big a sin as keeping a combine waiting. If the trailer was too close and nearly full, the corn cascaded over the side for what seemed an eternity before it was possible to widen the gap between trailer and combine harvester, and if the gap was too wide the grain poured from the spout onto the ground. Sometimes, as the load increased, a hasty missed gear change allowed the combine to romp away, the grain bouncing off the canvas roof and tin bonnet of the tractor like a miniature hailstorm.

I soon became quite proficient, but to start with the combine drivers were wary of their student, keeping a strict watch on the proceedings and a hand on the lever ready to shut down the auger at the first sign of trouble. Later, they hardly bothered to glance at me, concentrating on driving their combines, occasionally looking across to check the trailer was not overflowing, and I took this as a compliment. Jack and Alan were conscientious and alert, but Wilf often retreated into his dream world and it was not always easy to attract his attention to an overflowing trailer, and I soon found I had to be more alert to Wilf than he was to me.

On my very first trip to the dryer, I backed the trailer to the low wall of the pit and Fred came round to see me. He watched me tip the trailer, the oats rushing out into the concrete-lined pit with a satisfying swishing noise, the overstressed tyres resuming their normal profile making the trailer stand up an inch or two, as though glad to be rid of its load. I pulled forward and jumped off the tractor.

'I'll tell you two things, Davy,' said Fred. 'First, if that pit's empty when you comes to tip, give us a shout 'cos if the slide's open at the bottom an' you tips, you'll bung the works up an' we'll 'ave to clear it all by 'and. Second, don't forget to shut your tailboard when you's finished else you'll find corn goin' everywhere when you gets back to the field, and you won't be the first to 'ave done that.'

All this alarming advice resolved itself as the harvest progressed, but it was useful to be reminded for I had no wish to shut the dryer down for several hours because I had forgotten to check with Fred whether the slide, which controlled the flow of grain, was open or closed.

We finished the oats and made a start on the barley and I quickly discovered the intense irritation caused by the barley halms – the hard little stalks at the end of each grain, called barley 'hams' by the farm workers.

These halms found their way into every crevice of the body, setting up an itching as real as the imagined itching of ringworming. It was not always possible to take the corn from a combine upwind, and emptying one downwind was a nightmare; great clouds of dust enveloped the tractor and combine, and the little halms swirled around in the breeze, homing in with deadly accuracy on the eyes, hair and down the back of the shirt, from where they worked their way to the lower parts of the body. There was no escape, even with the canvas sides of the cab in place and the back rolled down. There were no cabs at all on the combines.

The harvest progressed in fits and starts, some barley being ready and some still in need of the sun's warmth before it was fully ripened. It was several days before we were in full swing.

'I 'ates the beginning of 'arvest,' Luke grumbled as we were topping sacks together in the dryer one afternoon. 'You never knows where you stands. One minute you's flat out combining an' thinking you's really stuck in, an' the next minute you's back to ordinary farm work, waiting for the corn to get fit again afore you can restart. What makes it worse is when you's stopped, all the other farms is combining.'

Mr. Chubb overheard Luke's complaining.

'Why do you think I always sow a small field of oats, Luke?' he asked.

'I doesn't know, Mr. Chubb, but I's often wondered,' Luke replied.

'Well, I'll tell you why. No one round here grows oats and our oats are always ready ahead of the barley. When we start combining them all the neighbours put their heads over the hedge, thinking we are at the barley and wondering where they have gone wrong. So they rush back and start combining unfit barley. They get in a terrible mess, bunged up combines, dryers going full blast all night, everyone bad tempered. They fall for it every year. And what do we do? I will tell you what we do. We wait until the barley's fit and go dung cart instead.'

'I wonders about Mr. Chubb sometimes,' Luke said after he had gone. 'I wonders 'ee's any friends at all the way 'ee carries on.'

❧

The harvest settled down to a steady routine, controlled by the weather as surely in the 1960's as it was when man first knocked the grain from an ear of corn. We started at about ten o'clock, depending how heavy the dew had been and finished when the dew rose again at about eight o'clock. Brian, Desmond and I maintained our rotation through to the following day, and if I had tipped the last load the previous evening I was last on the rota the next morning. This was a half-hour I always savoured, leaning meditatively against the rear wheel of the tractor, chewing a stalk of barley, watching Brian and Desmond slowly following the combines up the field, waiting for the sudden spurt of dust as their trailers were filled, knowing it would soon be my turn to start the day's harvesting and there would be no more time to stand and stare until the dew rose in the evening.

It was never a problem to empty Jack and Alan's combines: I drove up to them when I judged the tanks were nearly full, and when I was in position the lever was pulled and the vibrating, clattering auger poured the corn into the trailer. Wilf, however, was more intractable. Whether it was a lingering resentment against the student, a demonstration of his authority as a combine driver, sheer bloody-mindedness or a perverted sense of humour was difficult to know, but Wilf was determined to make life as difficult as possible for me. When I neatly pulled alongside him, leaving plenty of room to relieve him of his load before the headland, he affected not to notice me until we had almost reached it, and only then would he start his auger which deposited a derisory heap of grain into the trailer, barely covering the floor, before Wilf turned it off to swing round and set off up the field again. This was annoying, as I had to pull out, wait for Wilf to complete his manoeuvre and start the whole process again.

It was easy to play Wilf at his own game. Having done the rounds of Jack and Alan I drove close to Wilf and switched off the engine. Learning from him, I ignored him. He briefly glanced at me and, reassured, continued along the field, concentrating heavily on his work. As he dwindled into the distance he soon became aware his corn carter was not following him, and he became agitated, looking back with increased frequency, always resuming his concentrated study of the corn in front of him. It was a game of bluff, and I played it to the limit with full and unwitting cooperation from Wilf. His next move was to wave his tartan cap slowly over his head – the cap that had once been a garish tartan but which was now coloured a dirty black with only the remnants of its former glory showing through the encrusted dirt after years of suffering under Wilf's outsize feet. Still I ignored him. Faintly, above the noise of the combine, I could hear Wilf calling, and although it was impossible to distinguish his words, I had little doubt what they were. When a small mound of grain appeared at the top of the tank I reluctantly started the tractor and drove slowly down the field, timing my arrival to coincide with the first grains falling over the edge of the tank onto the ground. Wilf, meanwhile, was endeavouring to steer his combine with one hand and reaching behind him to level the grain with the other. It was no easy task and his machine zig-zagged wildly along the barley as he transferred his attention from levelling to steering and back again, leaving the normally ruler-straight line of standing corn looking like the serrated edge of a saw.

There was no delay in Wilf starting the auger now, and although I could not hear him above the din of straining machinery, the frequent shaking of his fist gave me the satisfaction that perhaps the message was finally getting through.

But it hadn't; Wilf never connected my protest to his own obtuseness and it was quite by chance I overheard him say to Jack one morning 'That nipper's useless, bloody useless.'

Jack, who knew perfectly well what was going on, paused and replied 'If you was to use your head and not keep Davy waiting, I doubt you'll find 'ee'll do the same to you.'

I never had any more trouble from Wilf in the harvest field.

⟨⟩

The aptly named cinder track wound steeply up the side of a hill, the long grass on either side flattened by the passage of the wide combines and higher up on the banks, rosebay willow herb brightened the scenery as it had for centuries of harvests. The cinder track led to a fifty-acre field called Trenchground, a name which evoked thoughts of the First World War, though quite why a field set high in the downs acquired such a dreary name was a mystery. No one on the farm knew the origins of the more obscurely named fields, neither did they care. 'That's what they's always bin called,' was the inevitable answer to my query. It probably didn't matter, but it would have been interesting to know why Trenchground, Lyders, Winnals and Rumble

Hill Field were so called, and with fields becoming amalgamated to accommodate the increasingly large farm machinery, a part of rural history was being lost for ever. Red Barn Field – although no one could remember the red barn – Pheasant Field and the more recently named Doodlebug Field, complete with its crater, were easy to understand, but Trenchground always puzzled me.

We were halfway through combining Trenchground when things started to go wrong. Jack's machine expired within the first hour of the day's work. It was clearly a major breakdown, necessitating Cecil removing one of the driving wheels and lowering the combine onto blocks of wood to gain access to the cause of the trouble. I was learning that nothing to do with mechanics was as straightforward as it appeared, and by mid-afternoon Cecil's legs were still protruding from the combine as he lay flat on his back, grunting and muttering to himself, his spanners clinking as he worked, and I remembered Mr. Chubb's phrase, 'He really comes into his own at harvest time'. It was tedious for us corn carters, geared up for the rush and tear of the harvest and now finding ourselves waiting for our loads. We gave Cecil a wide berth, leaving him to his work, leaning against our trailers, chatting and speculating how much longer the unfortunate Cecil would be.

Coming back from the dryer later in the afternoon, I met the normally sedate Mr. Chubb hurtling round a corner flat out in his Land Rover, on the wrong side of the road. Shaken, I carried on and at the bottom of the steep cinder track I looked up. High on the downs was a plume of white smoke; it came from the direction of Trenchground. Driving through the gateway at the top of the track the smoke was thick and choking, fanned by a gentle breeze; there was an ominous out-of-control sharp crackling from the burning corn, and the smoke was now tinged black, accompanied by an acrid smell of burning rubber. Circling upwind I could see Wilf's combine burning furiously, the tyres belching great rolls of thick black smoke and orange-red flame, the barley alight all around it.

Worse, the wind was taking the fire rapidly towards Jack's stranded combine which was already becoming indistinct in the smoke, like a ship on a misty sea. Cecil was almost crying with frustration. 'I only 'ad 'alf an hour's work and I'd 'ave finished' he repeated endlessly.

We set to work like demons to fight that fire and save the combine, eyes pouring, hair singed by falling embers, smoking holes appearing in our clothing, and all around us the frightening crackling of the burning corn. Mr. Chubb and James returned in their Land Rovers laden with every spare body they could find, even Archie, Mr. Chubb's eighty-year-old gardener, piles of sacks and all the pitchforks they could muster. We beat the flames with the sacks until our arms threatened to leave their sockets, forked the cut straw into heaps to burn away from the striken harvester, channels of sweat from the effort and the intense heat running sootily down our faces. Suddenly, the fire was gone, racing down the field to the hedge, the blackened smouldering circle around the combine only five feet away, showing how desperately close the fight had been.

We beat out the rest of the fire with comparative ease. It had burnt a corridor about a hundred yards wide down to the hedge, which was some four hundred yards from the blackened smoking wreck that had been Wilf's combine, now a total loss. A build-up of straw behind the exhaust pipe was the cause of the fire.

'She just erupted on me an' went away that fast I couldn't do nothing' said Wilf. 'They poxy extinguishers ain't no good neither,' he added gloomily.

We stood around, aimlessly, despondently, smoking our cigarettes. It didn't seem to matter now. Cecil resumed his work and Alan trudged back to his combine, which he had parked well away from the fire.

'Where's Mr. Chubb?' asked Fred.

' 'Ee left with James about an 'alf hour ago,' replied Jack. ' 'Ee didn't say nothing to no one.'

'Same as I says, you, 'ee'd better think of something fast,' Fred went on, 'else we'll be 'arvesting at Christmas an' beyond.'

We heard the noise of an engine and looked round. Mr. Chubb's Land Rover was tearing through the blackened stubble raising a trailer of ash behind it; if nothing else, the fire had worked wonders for his driving. He pulled round in a semi-circle, slammed on the brakes and almost fell out of the door as he alighted.

'What's that boy doing?' he asked, indicating Alan, who had just resumed work. 'Someone go and stop him, we'll be doing no more combining today.'

He had a conspiratorial look about him, like a conjurer about to pull a white rabbit from an empty top hat. He flung down the tailboard of the Land Rover, and inside were three crates of beer which he dispensed with rare abandon. When we all had a bottle and had unscrewed the tops, he slid a hip flask from his pocket, beaming wickedly.

'Here's to all of us,' he announced dramatically, taking a mighty swig and advancing at the same time to Wilf. He jabbed him powerfully in the chest with his forefinger. 'I've found you a new combine – a brand new one,' he said triumphantly. 'It will be here tonight. Don't you go setting fire to it like the old one.' He paused for another swig from his flask.

'What 'appened to the fire brigade?' Fred suddenly asked him. Mr. Chubb

stood, rocking on the balls of his feet, staring at Fred.

'We didn't need the fire brigade,' he said, momentarily taken aback.

'If we had to wait for them, we would have lost Jack's combine. We can manage on this farm – we've proved that.' (Much later I learnt no-one had thought to ring the Fire Brigade in the general panic; Mr. Chubb was the supreme diplomat.)

'Now take those crates out of my Land Rover, finish them, and don't forget to take the empties back to the pub. You can book your overtime to nine o'clock, and we'll start afresh in the morning.'

'I doesn't know 'ow 'ee does it,' Fred remarked as he watched Mr. Chubb speeding out of the field. 'There just ain't no new combines to be 'ad in the middle of 'arvest. 'Ee must be some sort of magician. An' as for the fire brigade…' He wandered off, muttering to himself before sitting on one of Cecil's five gallon drums of oil to finish his beer.

I was discovering Mr. Chubb was an extremely forceful personality who was accustomed to having his own way. I didn't envy the machinery salesman who had been on the receiving end of his request for a new combine at such a time.

I was also discovering the force of my mother's personality when I was made to strip to my underpants on the back lawn before I was allowed to walk up the stairs, which she had covered with newspaper, to take my bath.

It had been a long day.

ℭ

We were much better organised for our next fire. About a week later I was driving out of the field with a full load of barley when something caught my attention. Whether it was a faint reflected flicker on the windscreen or a barely heard but well remembered crackle from the burning corn I shall never know, but I looked round. Wilf, driving his brand new combine, out of sight of anyone else, was sedately working his way across the field, blissfully unaware that the straw falling from the rear of his machine was on fire. There was a gap of about ten yards between the fiercely burning straw and Wilf, and the gap was rapidly diminishing. I knew instantly what had happened. Wilf kept a supply of ready rolled cigarettes in his tin, and after I had unloaded him he had lit one of these, flicked his match over his shoulder and continued on along the field.

Turning round I raced back up the slope towards Wilf, flashing the one headlight that worked and futilely blowing the Fordson's feeble horn, but Wilf was supine, lost in his thoughts, occasionally drawing on his cigarette, the smoke drifting behind him to join the thicker white smoke of the burning straw. The trailer was swaying and lurching alarmingly behind, spilling corn from the sides and the old Fordson was straining, driven to the limit. It was not until I was about twenty yards from the dreaming Wilf that he noticed me, the burning swath of straw lapping the rear of his combine. I pointed behind, and Wilf stood up and looked round, for an instant refusing to believe what he saw. He lifted the header table, flung his cigarette to the ground and, ashen faced, turned his huge harvester downhill, making for the safety of the gateway. James, who was just driving into the field, took in the scene at a glance, reversed and roared away down the lane. In record time Harry, whom James had found making his way along the road towards the field with his baler, appeared with a plough and started ploughing a fire break – the baler was abandoned by the side of the road – and shortly after the Fire Brigade dramatically entered the field, the brass bell ringing in rhythm to the ruts.

'We can relax now,' said Brian as we paused from our beating of the flames with the familiar sacks, thoughtfully brought up to the field by James, 'they'll soon 'ave it out.'

He was wrong. The fire engine revved up its big diesel motor, the firemen holding the hose braced themselves, and to many shouts of 'Right' from the engine and answers of 'Right' from the men at the hose end, a tiny dribble of water trickled from the nozzle, barely dampening the earth. There was, apparently, a problem with the pump. To ribald shouts of derision from the farm workers – they all knew the part-time firemen well – and streams of obscenities from the fire crew, we wearily resumed our beating. Harry's fire break had contained most of the flames, and by the time the pump had been sorted out we had nearly extinguished the fire. The abashed firemen dampened down the corn, reeled up their hoses and departed.

'I bets that Wilf were smoking an' started the fire,' said Jack. 'Was you, Wilf?'

Wilf, still white-faced, shook his head and denied it.

'What about you, Davy. You must 'ave seen, you was close enough. Was 'ee smoking?'

This was difficult, but ten years of private education was well ingrained in my mind.

'I never saw, Jack,' I lied. 'There was too much going on.'

Jack gave me a long stare, and said nothing. I didn't dare look at Wilf.

'Mr. Chubb were right about one thing,' said Alan. 'We never did need they firemen. We can 'andle it on this farm. 'Ee's right about most things come to think of it.'

No one answered him.

C3

I was preparing to climb into the old Morris Minor that evening to go home when Mr. Chubb came out from the shadowy doorway of Fred's feed mill. There was no one else in the yard.

'I am not going to ask you whether or not Wilf was smoking,' he said, 'because I know what your answer will be, and only you and Wilf know the truth. Wilf denies it, naturally, and you will be evasive in that public school tradition of yours.' He jabbed me in the chest with his forefinger, a mannerism he used when he wanted to emphasise a point. 'I will tell you this. I know Wilf was smoking, I know it was his match that started the fire and I know you saw him smoking. You are here to learn in your eighteen months on this farm, so I will tell you what I am going to do. Wilf was born in the village, went to school here, married a village girl and his children were born in the village. I have known him all his life and, what is more, he has worked for me since he left school. He's learnt his lesson – he'll never smoke in the harvest field again and I doubt anyone else will after today. So I am not going to sack him or even mention the matter again for he has already had his punishment, and you want to remember that.'

He turned to go. My mother's car caught his eye, covered in dust.

'That car is a disgrace. Have it cleaned before your mother gets onto me. I couldn't cope with her at the moment.'

CS

True to his word, Mr. Chubb didn't sack Wilf but the following day he sacked Jack. It was just before lunchtime – or dinnertime as the farm workers called it – when James and Cecil were preparing for their lunchtime stint on two of the combines. Mr. Chubb was having a furious altercation with Jack over some setting on his machine and Jack, in his quiet but firm manner, was standing his ground. Mr. Chubb, red in his cherubic face, suddenly stalked off to his Land Rover, slammed the door and drove off, while Jack calmly walked across to James's Land Rover which we used to return to the farm at lunchtimes. Easing his lanky frame into the outside front seat, he closed the door and Alan let out the clutch. Desmond leant forward from the back.

'What 'appened, Jack?' he asked.

Jack, looking to his front, smiled to himself. 'The old bugger sacked me,' he said.

'You ain't going to take no notice of that?' asked Alan.

'I just might,' replied Jack. 'The garden needs doing, an' it's a nice day an' it's about time Mr. Chubb were taught 'ee cain't shout an' scream at 'is men an' always get away with it.'

Returning to the harvest field after lunch, we called at Jack's cottage. He was hoeing his vegetables.

'You coming?' asked Alan. Jack leant on his hoe. 'No I ain't,' he said. 'I've too much work to do 'ere.' He resumed his hoeing.

Mr. Chubb came into the field shortly after we restarted. Seeing Jack's idle combine parked on the headland, he turned to us.

'Where's Dingwell?' he demanded.

'You sacked 'im just afore dinner, Mr. Chubb,' Brian answered dryly. 'Doesn't you remember?'

'We'll soon see about that,' he said, getting into his Land Rover.

Ten minutes later he was back in the field, with Jack, who started up his combine and continued where he had left off before lunch: no more was said about the setting of his machine.

At tea time Jack told us what had happened. Mr. Chubb had found him still hoeing his vegetables. He walked up Jack's garden path and stopped close to him.

'What are you doing, Dingwell?' he had asked.

'I'm 'oeing my cabbages, Mr. Chubb,' Jack had replied.

'Why aren't you in the harvest field?'

'Because you sacked me, Mr. Chubb.'

138

Mr. Chubb took a step towards Jack and put an arm around his shoulders.

'You know I didn't mean that, Dingwell. You have worked for me for over thirty years; you should know me by now. Get in the Land Rover and we'll go back to the field.'

Jack laid down his hoe, collected his lunch box containing his flask and sandwiches, and sat in the Land Rover next to Mr. Chubb.

'You mustn't take any notice of me at harvest time,' he said. 'We all say things we don't mean when we are working hard.'

'I didn't,' Jack told us, happily chewing on one of his sandwiches, 'but it were about time the old bugger were taught he couldn't take nothing for granted.'

CR

We finished the barley and started the wheat, the wheat which was so much less itchy than the irritating barley, and which was so much denser. The extra weight was noticeable in the trailer – the Fordson had to be dropped down an extra gear to climb the dryer hill – and it was noticeable in the sacks, which were now two-and-a-quarter hundredweights instead of the two hundredweights of barley which had previously occupied the same space. I admired the sweating lorry drivers' strength as they loaded these heavy sacks and I sweated in my turn when we topped them in the dryer and in the old farrowing sheds. I was glad I had had my bet with Fred over a sack of barley; I would never have won it with a sack of wheat.

It was probably the extra weight that caused a puncture in a rear tyre of my Fordson Major – the weight from the trailer was transferred to the rear wheels via the drawbar for adhesion. I found the tyre deflated one morning when I went to the tractor shed.

'You look after my tractor, nipper,' said Wilf – for it was his tractor I was using – 'else I'll 'ave yer an' so will Cecil an' Mr. Chubb.' He seemed quite himself again, I reflected, since he realised Mr. Chubb wasn't going to sack him.

Cecil was unamused. 'I 'ates punctures in the middle of 'arvest,' he grumbled. 'I'll try and 'ave it done by dinner time, if nothing more goes wrong.'

'You'll have to take one of the Dextas,' James told me. 'I don't like these light tractors towing heavy loads of corn, so you will have to be extra careful.

The Dexta had a tremendous turn of speed for a tractor and, rounding a corner on the main road as I returned to the harvest field, I saw a six-wheeled lorry struggling slowly up the incline, its bulky load neatly sheeted down. It was too good an opportunity to miss. I opened the hand throttle to its maximum and started to overtake, the Dexta slowly gaining on the lorry. When I drew level with the cab, the driver glanced down at me briefly and then took another look, twisting in his seat, half leaning out of the window, his eyes goggling with disbelief. It was more than his pride could bear and he reached down and pushed the cold-start button – a device for pumping extra diesel into the cylinders. A great cloud of black smoke belched from the exhaust, and for a while we were thundering up the hill neck and neck, the lorry driver hunched over his steering wheel, whilst I pulled hard on the hand throttle trying to extract an extra half a mile an hour from the Dexta. From time to time we stared menacingly at each other and resumed our positions, locked in combat on our tortoise-like progress up the slope.

The brow of the hill defeated me and I was forced to drop back and tuck in behind the lorry which was still shoving out filthy black smoke from its rear. My last sight of the driver's face was in his mirror, triumphantly grinning with two tombstones of teeth hanging from his upper jaw, the only ones he possessed.

Cecil was as good as his word and my tractor was parked outside his workshop after lunch, its puncture repaired. There was, however, something not quite right, for the tractor seemed to have a pronounced lean to the left. Closer examination revealed there were eighteen inches of tyre at the bottom which had failed to come onto the rim. Cecil came out of his workshop rubbing his hands with cleanser, most of which was falling on the concrete.

'I tried everything to get that tyre back on the rim, Davy,' he said, 'bars, sledges an' levers, but she wouldn't 'ave it. I even tried this,' he said, holding out his dripping hands. 'I parked 'er like that in case it popped out, but it ain't. You does a few miles an' she'll come out alright,' he said confidently.

It never did. It was a curious sensation driving that tractor on the road, lurching to the left every time that portion of the tyre adrift from the rim made contact with the surface, and when I jumped off the tractor after a lengthy spell aboard, I found myself limping for a short time in sympathy with it, rather like stepping off a ship onto dry land after a long voyage and finding the ground moving in the motion of the swell. In addition the green oil light was permanently on, its penetrating beam distractingly shining in my eyes.

'It's only the switch,' Cecil told me.

I hoped he was right.

CB

The corn poured into the dryer from the fields at a terrific rate, far faster than the dryer could manage. The weather had been perfect for harvesting – little dew in the mornings – enabling earlier starts, fewer breakdowns and long sunny days and evenings with hardly a break for rain. Mr. Chubb drove around with a beam on his face, stopping me in the lanes to ask the inevitable 'Have you got your sheet and how many loads' – though the former seemed irrelevant at the moment – and spending his time between the harvest field and the dryer. The beam left his face midway through the afternoon when the dryer became clogged with corn. The antiquated equipment was simply inadequate for the advances that had been made in the harvesting machinery and couldn't handle the increased volume of corn. The result, at about three-thirty every afternoon, was an overflowing pit, an irritable Mr. Chubb and a truculent Fred.

'Same as I says, you, I keeps telling 'im if I opens 'er out any more she'll all jam solid, but 'ee won't believe me,' Fred said. ' 'Ee should 'ave ripped all this old stuff out years ago an' put in modern machinery. 'Ee won't listen, that's 'is trouble, an' now we's in the middle of 'arvest 'ee frets an' 'ee forgets. I told 'im two year ago when we got the extra combine my dryer would never 'ave it. An' look at it now.'

This was true. We tried backing through the thick layer of corn overflowing from the pit and half tipping the trailer before knocking out the pins on the tailboard in an attempt to shoot at least some of the corn over the back, but this did the trailers no good at all and achieved little respite.

The only answer was to resort to the grain shovel, a wide-ended aluminium shovel designed to lift the maximum amount of grain with the minimum of damage. It was hard work shovelling that grain into the pit and after about a quarter-of-an-hour it was depressing to look at an enormous heap of corn, piled ridiculously high, waiting for a sign that the auger buried beneath it was working. Slowly, like a handful of sand slipping between the fingers, the wheat could be discerned moving, jerkily at first, shaking itself down, then more positively, forming a small crater, slowly widening in circumference. Then it was time to shovel again.

We filled all the spare trailers and parked them under cover for the night shift – run by Sam and Luke – to empty, but that gave little breathing space: it was always back to the demanding shovel. There was a feeling of helplessness when, parked by the pit with a full load of corn, the deep exhaust beat of Desmond or Brian's tractors could be heard as one or other ascended the steep dryer hill. There was also a feeling of hopelessness when eventually returning to the field, we were confronted with three combines stopped in different positions, their tanks heaped up and overflowing with grain in exactly the same way as the inadequate dryer. It was a dreadful waste of the weather.

Mr. Chubb employed two youths from the village to shovel, but they were useless, preferring to stand around talking and smoking illicit cigarettes than working. They treated Brian, Desmond and I with ill-concealed contempt, not condescending to make even a token attempt to carry out the job for which they had been employed. Mr. Chubb soon sacked them.

'Same as I says, you, they never was no bloody good, neither was their fathers,' said Fred. 'If that's what's coming to replace us old 'uns, there ain't no bloody 'ope at all.'

ଔ

A flushed Mr. Chubb came round to the back of the dryer with Fred one afternoon where Brian and I were waiting to tip our trailers, gloomily watching the corn slowly sinking down in the pit.

'Tip your loads on the concrete apron,' he said, 'and go back up the field. I have been talking to the Old Man (even Mr. Chubb referred to him as 'The Old Man') and we are going to rip the dryer apart in the winter and install a completely new system. In the meantime we will take a chance with the weather, tip the corn here and Sam can use the foreloader at night to move it. That way it will be clear when we start in the morning and you won't have to do any more shovelling.'

' 'An' what if it rains?' asked Fred. 'There'll be a tidy drop of grain to spoil out there.'

Mr. Chubb clasped an arm around Fred's shoulders. 'It won't rain, Fred,' he said. 'I know that. The weather is set fair for weeks now; you mustn't trouble yourself about that, and besides, it's my worry, not yours.'

'An' I knows who'll get the blame if we gets a thunderstorm an' you 'as to shovel all that wet corn into the dell,' said Fred, freeing himself from Mr. Chubb's grasp and returning to the depths of his dryer.

'Wonderful man, Fred,' said Mr. Chubb, 'but he does get in a state at harvest time.'

ଔ

The new system worked well. There were no more hold-ups in the field, tipping the grain ceased to be the drudgery of idle waiting at such a busy time and, as Mr. Chubb had forecast, the weather held.

'I doesn't know 'ow 'ee gets away with it,' said Fred, taking off his cap and slowly shaking his head. 'Same as I says, you, 'ee gets away with things 'ee's no right to, then 'ee crows to 'is friends an' tells 'em they should 'ave done as 'ee done. You doesn't want to take no notice of 'ee, Davy, 'ee'll only learn you the way not to farm.'

I gently reminded Fred, as a gambling man, that Mr. Chubb was really taking far less chance than we were on our daily cross doubles.

'If 'ee did the 'orses, 'ee'd be a millionaire with 'is luck,' he replied. It was difficult to disagree.

☙

Mr. Chubb hired the local coal merchant's lorry and men for carting the bales and moving the sacks of grain from the dryer to the old farrowing sheds. They were a cheerful lot, those three coalmen. They lived in the same village as Fred, two miles from the farm and, freed from grime and coal dust, were almost unrecognisable from the blackened men who delivered the fuel in the grim winter months with such short daylight hours. They regarded this work almost as a holiday, carrying the heavy sacks of corn and stacking them with an ease I envied, pitching bales high onto the lorry and, crammed tight in the cab driving the often, to my inexperienced eye, dangerously overloaded, swaying vehicle across the field to the barn.

Norman and Henry, when they had finished the milking, hitched a trailer to my Ferguson and, looking out of place away from the milking parlour driving an unfamiliar tractor, loaded bales until dusk. Exchanging insults with the coalmen, they worked with casual abandon and, watching them drive their untidily laden trailer out of the field, I wondered the bales stayed on at all. It was noticeable that the ever-willing Henry pitched the bales whilst Norman took the relatively easy job of stacking, sitting down for a breather each time Henry moved the tractor on; but Henry was the under-cowman.

'Pair of bloody amateurs,' observed Cecil one evening. 'They's no right to earn extra overtime with their pay.'

It was the well worn cry, but every bale in the barn was a bale saved from the weather, and I was surprised at Cecil's comment and said so.

'They should be in bed so they's fresh for milking in the morning, not playing around up 'ere doing everyone out of overtime,' he replied. 'They thinks they's above us, like a pair of primanonnas.'

☙

The harvest was nearly completed, the weather had held and the barns were filled with bales of straw, bales for feeding, bales for bedding and bales for building the lambing pens in the spring. The coalmen were still moving sacks of corn out of the dryer on their lorry, Norman and Henry had resumed their normal routine in the dairy, ending the eternal grumbling about their overtime, and all the surplus straw was burnt. Pal had parked his bagging combine in one of the sheds, Harry had put away his baler and they began the winter ploughing, Pal condemned to his long exile on his crawler tractor. Although it was still high summer, winter started early on the farming calendar.

We finished our penultimate field one Saturday evening, leaving a sixty-acre field of wheat to be cut the following day to complete the harvest.

'I reckons we'll finish it tomorrow, with a bit of luck,' said Jack, 'an' then we can start on the taters.'

There seemed no end to this harvesting business.

Wilf and Cecil went out that Saturday night, prematurely celebrating the end of the harvest and on the Sunday morning the effects of innumerable pints of brown and mild were clearly evident. Cecil spoke to no one, communicating in grunts, his sallow skin and dark eyes failing to disguise his fragility. Wilf turned up a quarter of an hour late, and he looked terrible, even his bushy black beard not concealing his gigantic hangover. Mr. Chubb gave him a penetrating look and settled for 'Good morning, Wilf'. It was difficult to reprimand someone for being late on a Sunday morning and, besides, Mr. Chubb knew his men well. I resolved to keep well away from Wilf and his hangover, and I didn't envy him driving a noisy, dusty, vibrating combine harvester in his condition.

We fuelled the combines with jerrycans of diesel drawn from the bomb, greased them and moved to the last field, a mile and a half away. I led the procession down the main road, driving astride the white line with the one functioning headlight of the Fordson glaring a cycloptic warning to the sparse traffic. The three combines followed with Brian and Desmond at the rear, and we soon arrived at the field.

Jack carefully manoeuvred his machine through the gateway with a couple of inches to spare each side, but Wilf, hardly surprisingly, had difficulty aligning his combine. Mr. Chubb pulled his handkerchief from his top pocket and, bending low, waved it left or right to guide Wilf through. After his third attempt, with Mr. Chubb waving his handkerchief in his left hand, his right arm stretched parallel to the ground, his knees flexed, looking like a man in charge of taxiing an aircraft, Wilf had had enough. He climbed down the steps of the combine with an alacrity which surprised us all and stalked over to Mr. Chubb.

'If you thinks you can drive this bloody thing better than I,' he said, 'then you'd best get up there an' take it through the gateway yourself, an' I'll 'ave your bloody hanky an' wave you into the field.'

Mr. Chubb was devastated. He returned the handkerchief to his top pocket and turned to face us.

'I do believe I have upset Wilf,' he said.

ଔ

We finished that field at eight o'clock, the last field of the 1961 harvest, and mine was the last load to be tipped in the dryer. We stood and talked as

Jack drove alongside my trailer and augered out the dregs from his tank, then he switched off his engine and there was a miraculous peace. Three and a half weeks of dust, heat, long hours and hard work had ended for another year. I started my engine and prepared to leave the field.

' 'Ang on a minute, nipper,' said Wilf. 'I wants a run out.'

We were parked in front of a row of farm cottages and there were women and children in the gardens. Wilf shielded himself from view behind my trailer. It was too good an opportunity to miss. I waited until Wilf was well underway – he was looking over his shoulder, talking to Jack – and slowly released the clutch. I was twenty yards from Wilf when the penny dropped, too far to hear what he said as he desperately turned himself through one hundred and eighty degrees, but I had little doubt of what it was. It had not been a good day for Wilf.

10.

End of the Farming Year

After the end of harvest, I resumed my weekly lunches with Mr. Chubb. These lunches seldom served their original purpose for discussing farming, but at our first post-harvest lunch I was determined to ask Mr. Chubb's opinion of it. He was mixing us a couple of his lethal cocktails, and he turned and thrust mine into my hand.

'Sit down and I will tell you,' he said. He took a deep swallow from his glass, placed it on the table and leant forward to me. 'It was a wonderful harvest, one of the best I have known since I started farming nearly seventy years ago. (I doubted the veracity of the seventy years ago; it was an extravagant claim even by Mr. Chubb's standards.) It was the best yield we have ever had on this estate, the weather was perfect and we barely had a hitch. It was the harvest of a lifetime.' He beamed at me from behind his drink. 'You all did wonderfully well.'

I thought of the two fires, the lost combine, the breakdowns, the trouble tipping at the dryer and the chance he took with the weather and said as much to Mr. Chubb. He waved his hand dismissively.

'Nothing,' he said, 'they were nothing at all. The thing that matters at harvest time is the corn, and we fetched it in with a record yield. That's what counts in this business as you will find out when you have your own farm. There will be a good bonus in your pay packets this week. I have spoken to the Old Man and the Major and you will all have a smile on your faces this Friday. I look after my men here, and they know it and stay with me longer than any men on any farm in the county.'

It was a familiar boast, and Mr. Chubb, mightily pleased with himself, retired to the cocktail cabinet again. He brought the drinks back to the table and settled down firmly in his chair. Leaning forward, jabbing the air expansively in the vicinity of my chest with his index finger, he said 'It's our harvest supper the Saturday after next in the village hall, and you will be coming to that. You can bring your parents if you like,' he added as an afterthought.

I declined the invitation on my parents' behalf – I never told them it had been issued – for I had little idea of what the harvest supper entailed and the thought of my parents meeting Wilf well into his cups, or conversing with Fred with his outrageously colourful vocabulary, frankly appalled me. The stories they would be told about their son's progress were too awful to contemplate, and there was still the small matter of my smoking, about which, I thought, they knew nothing, although experience had taught me it was difficult to fool my mother for long.

I was enjoying myself working for Mr. Chubb and I was reluctant to jeopardize my chances of continuing to work for him by introducing my parents to a way of life I suspected they hardly knew existed.

ᘗ

I was working in the dryer with Fred soon after the harvest, our hours telescoped back to normal. It seemed odd knocking off at five o'clock and having the whole evening free. There was a sneaking guilt at not working late and resuming normal hours.

'Same as I says, you,' Fred announced, 'I likes this time of year, the 'arvest done an' the farming year ending, an' we can take things easier.'

I, too, liked the autumn, the cool refreshing mornings, the low haze hanging over the valleys and the damp sweet smell of the earth. I was curious about Fred's last remark and asked him when the farming year started.

'It starts with 'tatering in a few weeks time,' he replied decisively.'

'It ends with the 'arvest supper an' starts again with 'tatering.'

The beginning of the farming year was something that had puzzled me for some time. The potato farmers' year, I would have thought, started with the planting, not the harvesting of the crop, the sheep farmers' year when the rams were put to the ewes, and the corn farmers' year when the winter ploughing started, which was immediately after harvest. On a mixed farm the start of the cycle of the main crop, to my mind, should indicate the start of the year. It was a small point, but Fred was adamant that the potato harvest began the farming year on Mr. Chubb's farm. It was useless to point out that potatoes formed only a small part of the farm's rotation, or that corn was the main crop; Fred would not move from his view.

'Same as I says, you, it's always been the 'tatering 'ere, an' as long as Mr. Chubb grows 'em, it always will be.'

ᘗ

The young farmers club meetings, suspended for the duration, like my weekly lunches with Mr. Chubb, resumed when the harvest was completed.

At our first post-harvest meeting we were informed there was a ploughing match arranged for the following week and, furthermore, it included a young farmers class. It was the week before the harvest supper.

In the past, the young farmers class had always been poorly supported, partly because it was not always easy to procure a tractor and plough, and partly because young farmers tended to enjoy spectating rather than participating on days out. There were too many people to talk to and too much to do without the bother of taking part. Our chairman was unyielding; the ploughing match must be supported and, moreover, he had a trump card for he had managed to borrow a tractor and plough. All he needed was a volunteer, and the excuses offered that evening were almost beyond belief. I sat there smugly, secure in the knowledge I had never ploughed a furrow in my life, but somehow the discussion centred on myself. Startled, I protested, but in vain, and unwittingly, I found myself the sole representative of our club in the ploughing match.

'Listen,' said Geoffrey, our chairman. 'You are the only person available. It's not important you haven't ploughed before, but we must be represented. You will have plenty of help. Derek (one of our 'older' young farmers) has promised to give you every assistance, and there really is nothing to it.'

He sounded desperate and I was more than doubtful.

'I might not be able to get the day off,' I said.

'I know Mr. Chubb,' said Geoffrey. 'There will be no problem there.'

CB

I tackled Mr. Chubb about it the next day.

'Wonderful idea,' he said. 'Of course you can have the day off. I shall be there myself, presenting the prizes, and I have entered Wilf in the competition as well. You both will bring back cups to the farm.'

There was no salvation there, and I doubted the cups. With my ignorance and Wilf's temper I wondered at Mr. Chubb's judgement. Wilf was aghast when I told him.

'You cain't plough, nipper,' he said. 'Takes years to learn to plough. Cain't learn it from no book neither.'

I mumbled something about having help.

'Against the rules,' he replied. 'You'll be disqualified.' He stomped off, his professional pride hurt at the thought of the farm student competing in the same competition.

CB

I had to collect the tractor and plough from the far side of a small town. Driving back in the morning rush hour with a three-furrow plough on the back was no easy task, for the motorists, eager to arrive at their desks, had no conception of the law of physics which decreed a three-furrow plough swung round on its own arc when turning. Horns were sounded and cars moved rapidly out of the way when their drivers realised the plough might scratch their cossetted vehicles.

I drove into the field, close to the banks of the same river which threaded its way through Mr. Chubb's farm, without the remotest idea of what was required of me. The field was alive with tractors of all descriptions – crawler tractors trailing impossibly long ploughs supported by a wheel at the rear, vintage tractors, horses, pulling single-furrow ploughs and the everyday working tractors from nearly every farm in the district. Spectators wandered through the stubble of the recently harvested field, and officials from the Growmore Club, who were organising the event, directed participants to their respective areas to plough, according to their class. There was a beer tent, filled with my young farmer friends who had made their various excuses for not competing and there was a refreshment van run by a man who was reputed to possess the strongest bladder in the county. He regularly turned up at shows, ploughing matches and sales, never for a moment leaving his van.

Derek found me and wordlessly made some vigorous adjustments to my plough

'Follow me,' he commanded, 'and I'll show you where your pitch is.'

He led me to the area I had to plough, tucked well away from the main events; evidently the young farmers did not rate too highly with the organisers, but it suited me. The last thing I wanted was a crowd of critical spectators watching a young farmer farm student trying his hand at ploughing for the first time.

'I think I have set the plough about right,' Derek said. 'Now you see that big oak tree in the hedgerow? Aim for that.'

I lowered the plough and set off. Aiming for the oak tree proved more difficult than I imagined. Constantly turning around to check the unfamiliar plough, I veered off-course and missed the oak tree by at least six feet. It was not an auspicious start.

'Never mind,' said Derek, 'You'll have to do the best you can.' He moved off hastily as the judges approached. This bad start proved impossible to correct, and the more I ploughed the more the original error was compounded. My friends, when the judges were not in evidence, freely offered advice and Derek kept a close eye on my progress, occasionally adjusting the plough for me when no one was watching. Eventually I finished ploughing my cockeyed patch and anxiously awaited the judges' verdict. I came third, which was hardly surprising as there were only three entries in the class and a beaming Mr. Chubb handed me an envelope which contained a one pound note, and a certificate. Wilf came nowhere.

'It ain't right,' he told me, 'with all that 'elp you gets an' you wins a pound. I's been ploughing since I were a nipper an' gets nothing. You should 'ave been disqualified.'

The local paper reported the ploughing match. Young Farmers class (entries five) it stated, and gave my name as third placed. Wilf, for once, was speechless.

○✗

'Same as I says, you, I'd enjoy the 'arvest supper if it weren't for that bloody vicar,' Fred told me. 'Mr. Chubb will insist on 'aving 'im there every year an' 'ee spoils it for us – we cain't talk proper amongst ourselves in case we upsets 'ee with a bad word, an' you knows me, Davy, after a couple of drinks I finds it 'ard to control my tongue.'

This was news to me. Fred was by far the most accomplished user of bad language I had ever heard in my life, drunk or sober.

'Why 'ee 'as to bring religion into it an' 'alf ruin our evening I cain't work out. The old bugger mumbles grace an' then 'ardly says a word to us lot. Still,' he said, brightening, ' 'ee's usually gone early, an' that's a blessing.'

There was, I suspected, little love lost between the vicar and Fred. Brian, Fred and I were walking across the narrow brick bridge which spanned the stream one morning when we encountered him coming the other way, head bent, hands clasped behind his back, unaware of us. Fred wished him a cheerful good morning adding, in his adjectival manner, what a nice morning it was. The vicar, who was more at home with elderly ladies drinking Earl Grey from delicate porcelain cups than administering the needs of his more rough and ready parishioners, faltered, but Fred happily continued across the bridge.

'Does you know what you said to 'im?' asked Brian in disbelief.

'I wished 'ee a good morning,' Fred replied, surprised.

'You did more than that,' said Brian. 'You wished 'un too good a morning.'

Fred denied it strongly. 'I wouldn't speak to clerics like that,' he said sincerely. 'I respects 'em too much ever to use bad language in front of 'em.'

○✗

I turned up in good time for the harvest supper, for it was all part of my education and, besides, I was curious to meet the wives of the farm workers, most of whom I did not know. I was quite certain they had been fed stories of the farm student that bore little resemblance to reality, and I was hoping to correct the inevitable exaggerations before the beer took hold of their husbands and all was lost in my defence.

The mist was gently rising from the chalk stream flowing beside the village hall; it was a balmy late August evening and already early cock-

150

chafers were hurtling through the air, navigating with all the accuracy of inebriated fighter pilots, ricochetting clumsily off the building like fat whining bullets fired from primitive muskets.

If I thought I was early I was mistaken, for the hall was packed with people, many of whom I had never seen before, some of them already seated at the bare trestle tables, their pints of beer and ports and lemonade in front of them; these were the pensioners and their wives, many even older than Mr. Chubb's erratic claims to his age, and they easily outnumbered those currently employed on the estate. They were the men and their women who had lived in the days when the horse had ruled the farm, more important to it than the harvest itself.

The hall was a late Victorian building, typical of most village halls in the county, with a low stage at the far end and a kitchen to one side of the stage and, more importantly it appeared, a room to the other side (which was usually the doctor's surgery) containing two large barrels of beer and miscellaneous wooden crates of drinks. The Old Man and Mr. Chubb really looked after their staff, past and present. The high-pitched, bare-raftered roof was already filling with tobacco smoke, and on the stage there was a smaller trestle table, as yet unoccupied, which I guessed correctly was for the Old Man, Mr. Chubb, James, their wives and Fred's 'bloody vicar.'

Most people were dressed in their Sunday best, but there was one very small, very old man flitting between the tables, talking to everyone and listening to no one, helping himself to generous handfuls of crisps which had been placed in bowls at the elbows of the beer drinkers. He was dressed in a dirty old shirt, fastened at the top with a collar stud, a pair of stained trousers held up by a dangerously thin pair of braces and on his feet he wore a pair of hobnailed boots in which he skidded around the wooden floor, leaving deep grooves and threatening to upend himself at every turn.

I asked Fred who he was, 'That's the Colonel,' he told me, 'the most obstinate, cantankerous old man what's ever lived in this village. 'Ee were born 'ere, 'ee ain't never left 'ere an' 'ee'll die 'ere. You cain't tell 'im nothing an' if you tries 'ee goes an' does the opposite. I expect 'is missus told 'im to dress up smart for the 'arvest supper an' that's why 'ee looks a mess. 'Ee's well over ninety, as 'ard as nails an' 'ee's as deaf as a bloody post, but that don't matter 'cos 'ee ain't never listened to anything anyone's said in 'is whole life.'

Meanwhile The Old Man, Mr. Chubb, James and their wives, and the vicar who was a widower, had arrived. They had been at the Old Man's house for a pre-harvest supper drink. They circulated amongst the new and the old employees of the estate. Mr. Chubb beamed at me. 'I knew you would come,' he said. 'I knew you wouldn't let me down.'

I was startled, for I had no idea he considered I would absent myself from the harvest supper. In any case he had virtually ordered me to attend and I never intended missing it anyway. He introduced me to the Old Man who shook my hand warmly.

'I met your father once,' he said. 'A fine fisherman. I hope they are teaching you something on my farm.' This inconsequential conversation was the only one I held with the Old Man in all my time working on his farm.

Fred, rather bashfully, introduced me to his wife, Ethel. She was a short dumpy woman with merry brown eyes, and I guessed she kept Fred firmly under control at home.

'So you're Davy. I've heard all about you from my Fred,' she said.

'We've both said how funny it is that the farm's only two students are both called Davy. You wants to watch Fred, He'll either learn you good or he'll lead you right up the wrong garden path.'

I replied I thought he had probably done a little of both.

Desmond awkwardly introduced me to his girlfriend, Florence. They had been courting for a number of years, and I regarded her with awe. She was huge, wobbling shyly at Desmond's side like a monstrous jelly, threatening to dissolve into a pool of highly scented water on the floor in the hot atmosphere of the hall. She never said a word to me, merely smiling at her enormous feet, and when someone accidentally pushed me into her and I was thrust against her enormous bulk, I felt as though I was sinking into a great soft feather bed. There was no doubt Florence and Desmond were well suited to each other, and I thought they would produce some interesting children.

Brian's wife was a petite brunette. She was extraordinarily pretty, wearing a daring dress and high heels. She wasn't lacking in confidence like Florence and was the centre of attention wherever she stood. I noticed Mr. Chubb pointedly drew her into a long and involved conversation while openly observing her obvious charms.

'Wonderful girl, Pam,' he said, pausing as he passed by me. 'I have known her since she was a child, but I never thought she would turn out to be such a pretty girl.'

He drank deeply from his tumbler of whisky and continued on his way. Brian, only a few months older than me, had been married when I was still a schoolboy struggling with exams. Now he had a wife and young child while I had only just been let loose on the world. I felt I had a long way to go before I caught up Brian in the learning stakes.

The table on the stage was now occupied and the womenfolk were carrying steaming bowls of soup from the kitchen and placing them on the tables, but there was no sign of Wilf or Cecil.

'They's down at the bloody pub,' said Brian in answer to my enquiry. 'Beats me why they 'as to go there first, but they always does.'

As Brian was talking there was a tremendous cacophony outside the hall, a revving engine quickly killed, slamming doors and shouts and laughter.

'That's they now,' said Brian gloomily.

We were standing near the open doors of the hall and Wilf lurched in, grinning from ear to ear, closely followed by a tall dark-haired woman whose carelessly applied bright red lipstick accentuated the gruesome inadequacies of her dentistry. Wilf paused. 'Hello Bri,' he said, then, turning to me said, 'Meet the missus, Davy. 'Ere, Edna, you's 'eard me talk about the student, well 'ere 'ee is.'

There were no social niceties to Wilf. We shook hands rapidly and she shrieked to Wilf; 'Let's get a bloody drink. They's almost ready to sit down.'

Wilf and Edna barged their way through the crowd to the bar, shouting greetings, closely followed by Cecil and his morose and, from what I had heard, aptly named wife, Mona.

There were no specific places allocated for the harvest supper, and I rather thought I might sit next to Brian. Fred, however, had other ideas for me and I foolishly allowed myself to be lured outside for a moment on a false pretext, and when Fred and I returned there was only one seat left, between the Colonel and Sheila, Alan's unfaithful wife. There had been connivance at work here, and I regarded the prospect of sitting between these two with horror; the deaf colonel and Sheila (whom I had met before), obviously dragged reluctantly to the supper by Alan to keep up appearances.

'You sit down there an' enjoy yourself, Davy boy,' said Fred with a grin.' I cursed him inwardly and resolved to even the score with him later, but I knew this would be a hopeless task. Fred sat down at a table right at the end of the hall, next to the electricity meter, with a supply of shilling pieces with which to feed it during the evening.

'When the last 'un's gone,' I heard him say, slurping his soup, 'the party's over.'

But he had forgotten the grace. We rose to our feet, Fred hastily dropping his spoon into his soup bowl and wiping his mouth with the back of his hand as he stood, and the vicar, as Fred had predicted, head bowed, eyes closed, hands clasped, muttered several incomprehensible words which constituted the grace. He stood silent for a moment, swaying slightly, his eyes still tightly closed while we watched him for our cue to start the meal. Suddenly he opened his eyes, raised his hands and sat heavily on his chair. The harvest supper had started.

The food was magnificent, the best the farm workers' cottage gardens could produce, and the roast lamb that accompanied the delectable vegetables was succulent and fat ('I 'ates meat without a bit of fat,' Fred had once told me) but the company was trying. The Colonel laboured under the misapprehension that I was some relation of Mr. Chubb's and bellowing into his ear to correct his illusion caused much merriment at my expense and left me exhausted. His wife never said a word, and I couldn't blame her, for years of living with this deaf old bigot must have dulled her senses entirely. He spoke loudly and continuously, and it was my misfortune that I inescapably fascinated him. Food flew liberally from his mouth as he spoke and soon there was a covering on the table round his plate like confetti after a rainy wedding. The only relief was when he paused for a drink from his beer, and I tried to draw out the intractable Sheila, but this was an impossible task as she was monosyllabic, without conversation of any kind. Talking briefly to Alan while the women cleared the plates helped restore some sanity, and even then the Colonel continued to shout in my ear, undismayed by my ignorance of him. I reckoned he was so used to this that he regarded my rude behaviour as normal.

The beer flowed for the men and, mostly, the ports and lemonade for the women. The 'management' table, as Alan termed it, was whisky and wine. From time to time the lights went out and Fred, armed with a torch for just such an aberration, clambered onto a chair and fed more shilling pieces into the meter; Wilf and Edna were becoming louder by the minute. I noticed she was drinking gin and tonic rather than the standard port and lemon – and Cecil was sitting back in his chair, apparently comatose.

Mr. Chubb rose to his feet and banged the table. 'Christ, it's the bloody speech now,' said the Colonel in his abrasive voice. 'It's the same one every year.' Mr. Chubb glared at him but the Colonel was unabashed. He was also probably right, for Mr. Chubb repeated almost word for word his evaluation of the harvest at our last lunch. When he came to 'The best harvest I have ever known' the Colonel, his hearing miraculously restored, interjected contemptuously, 'it's always bin a good 'arvest on this farm, even when it's pissed down all summer.'

The tables were cleared, and the vicar scuttled off home to prepare himself for his tiny congregation in the morning, reflecting, no doubt, despite his calling, his relief that the Colonel was not counted amongst it.

Jack, a man of unsuspected talent, produced an accordion which he played with a lingering romanticism which, though sometimes melancholy, summarised the unspoken thought that the hot days of summer were over and the long slog of winter was beginning. When he played the well known tunes, the Colonel sang in a fine deep baritone which reverberated pleasingly around the hall. The old boy at least possessed one saving grace.

' 'Ow did you get on with the old bugger?' Fred asked me craftily. I told him in no uncertain tones.

'Well,' he said, 'same as I says, you showed an interest in 'im, so I thought it best you got to know 'im for yourself.'

ଔ

All the women were in the kitchen washing up the plates – there was no emancipation in this village – and from time to time Edna's raucous laughter stabbed into the hall like a thunderbolt, bouncing around the walls and eliciting the Colonel, of all people, to comment on the noise. The chairs had been moved back from the tables and the men were sitting in earnest groups, discussing the harvest and the past year, the tobacco smoke once again rising to the bare rafters, the carelessly held tankards slopping their contents unnoticed onto the floor.

Freed from the constraints of the awful colonel, I looked around the hall observing the little groups of farmworkers celebrating the end of the most important event in the farming calendar. Pal, Frank and Harry were sitting together. 'Never seen the like of it,' I heard Harry say. 'It's that bloody dry I can 'ardly get the plough in the ground, an' when I does there's great trails of dust behind me.' Pal nodded agreement, put his beer on a spare chair and laboriously started to roll a cigarette.

'I may be wrong, but I know I'm right,' he started, speaking the very thought that was in my mind as I watched him. Alan and Brian were leaning around the Colonel in animated conversation. The Colonel sat back between them in a rare silence, serenely smoking a pipe of ferocious pungency, staring at the ceiling, but it was Wilf who really caught my eye.

Mr. Chubb had descended from the stage and seated himself at the end of one of the long trestle tables, a full glass of whisky in his hand. Wilf, now in an advanced stage of inebriation, had pulled up a chair next to him and was holding a long, rambling and largely incomprehensible conversation with him. They were an incongruous pair, the immaculately dressed Mr. Chubb, his silver hair shining in the lights and his carefully knotted tie contrasting starkly with Wilf, his unfamiliar tie loosened and pulled askew, his collar undone and his hair standing on end from his habit of running his hands through it, back and forth, as if seeking his filthy tartan cap from which he was so seldom separated except in moments of anger and formal occasions. Suddenly, Wilf leant forward and put an arm around Mr. Chubb's shoulders.

'You's the best gaffer I's ever worked for,' he announced. 'I couldn't work for no one finer than you, Charlie.'

Mr. Chubb beamed with genuine pleasure despite the familiarity.

'I am the only person you have worked for Wilf,' he replied equably.

'But you's still the finest,' said Wilf, taking his arm from Mr. Chubb's shoulder in order to have a long pull at his beer.

೪

The evening was drawing to a close. The women were emerging from the kitchen holding mysterious biscuit tins and paper carrier bags containing leftovers and favourite utensils that had been used at harvest suppers for years and considered far superior to the best the village hall could provide. Jack had packed away his accordion and Fred was becoming increasingly erratic with his feeding of the meter, plunging us into longer and longer periods of darkness whilst he fumbled with his torch and the shilling pieces. The Old Man and his wife had left, nodding a silent farewell, and Mr. Chubb had returned to the management table where he gently helped Mrs. Chubb to her feet and passed her her handbag from beside the table leg. James, taking his cue from Mr. Chubb, helped his wife from her chair and they prepared to leave. Desmond and Florence had already sneaked away

'They's up to no good, they two,' Brian had informed me – and Wilf, his left arm crooked around the back of his chair, his right hand holding his beer, legs stretched out, was smiling inanely at the wall, completely content. His two large eye teeth were just visible under his beer-drenched moustache, with no other front teeth between them. He looked like a monstrous hairy baby.

Edna asked my unspoken question.

' 'Ow the bloody 'ell are we going to get the bugger 'ome?' she shouted. Cecil wordlessly slouched over and with Edna on one side – she was a strong girl – and Cecil on the other side, Wilf, his arms draped leadenly over their shoulders, was deposited on the front passenger seat of his Ford Prefect. Edna and Mona climbed into the back of the car and Cecil sat waiting in the driver's seat. When they had slammed the doors he pulled the self-starter and the car, already in gear, lurched out of the car park in a series of drunken leaps in empathy with its occupants and sped into the darkness, without lights, leaving a thick cloud of oily smoke and scattered gravel in its wake.

'I wonders 'ow they gets on,' said Brian. 'Wilf 'll 'ave an 'angover lasting till Monday afternoon if I knows 'im.'

I found out how they got on from Alan the following Monday morning. Alan lived next door to Wilf in a row of tied farm cottages about half-a-mile from the hall, and he recounted the story in the farmyard while we waited for Mr. Chubb and James to give us our orders for the day. There was no sign of Wilf.

'We 'eard these muffled bangs an' thuds,' he said, 'an' plentys of shouting, an' suddenly there were an almighty clang. The bugger 'ad fallen in the bath an' 'ee were yelling at Edna to 'elp 'im out, but she wouldn't. 'Ee were that drunk 'ee couldn't get out on 'is own. 'You got yerself in there,' she shouted, 'an' you can bloody well get yerself out. I'm going to bed.' We 'eard a few more bangs and scrabbling noises, then nothing. I do believe the bugger spent the night in that bath.'

At that moment Wilf came into the yard, and he looked terrible. He had a large waterproof plaster on his temple, doubtless as a result of his encounter with the bath, and his face was an unhealthy grey.

' 'Ow are you feeling this morning, Wilf?' enquired Brian cheerfully. 'You doesn't look too good – been at the beer again?' Wilf ignored him and Brian turned to Desmond. 'An' what 'appened to you, pushing off early with Florence on Saturday night? Did you get a little bit?'

Desmond shuffled his huge frame from foot to foot, staring hard at the muddy toecaps of his boots. Clearing his throat he looked up at us and said, 'Well, it were like this, see. I did an' I didn't.'

It had been an interesting harvest supper.

ભ

My original brief when I started working for Mr. Chubb was for a nine-month trial period – if I lasted that long – after which my progress was to be reviewed by Mr. Chubb before he allowed me to proceed with the second nine months, assuming my progress had met with his satisfaction.

The harvest supper coincided with the completion of my first nine months, and it worried me Mr. Chubb had not yet let me know whether or not I was to continue. My parents had not mentioned the matter, presumably hoping silence would solve everything, so at my first post-harvest supper lunch with Mr. Chubb I tackled him.

He sipped his drink, placed it on the table and leant back in his chair, his hands clasped across his stomach.

'I had quite forgotten about that agreement,' he admitted. He looked at me thoughtfully for a moment, leant forward in his chair and pointed his forefinger at me. 'You are enjoying yourself here,' he said, 'and the men like you. Do you wish to stay for a further nine months?'

I nodded.

He stretched back into his chair, picking up his glass on the way.

'Then there is nothing more to be said.'

THE END

COUNTRY BOOKSHELF
from Ex Libris Press presents the following books:

MARCH WINDS & APRIL SHOWERS
Country Weather Lore by Ralph Whitlock
80 pages; Illustrated with Bewick engravings; Price £3.50

THE SECRET LANE by Ralph Whitlock
A Country Story set in the 1930s.
152 pages; Price £4.95

LETTERS FROM THE ENGLISH COUNTRYSIDE
by Ralph Whitlock
Topics included here are firmly rooted in the traditional life of the
countryside. A nostalgic but wry view of the past is balanced by an often
humorous commentary on the present.
160 pages; Numerous pen & ink drawings; Price £4.95

CHRISTIANA AWDRY'S HOUSEHOLD BOOK
by Margaret Jensen
Recipes and cures selected from an eighteenth century household book.
128 pages; Pen & ink drawings; Price £4.95

GRAN'S OLD-FASHIONED REMEDIES, WRINKLES AND RECIPES
by Jean Penny
Remedies for common ailments; wrinkles, or tips, to save time and effort
about the house; recipes using inexpensive ingredients to create mouth-
watering dishes: all are included within these pages.
96 pages; Numerous engravings; Price £3.50

GRAN'S OLD-FASHIONED GARDENING GEMS by Jean Penny
Packed full of tips and details aimed at the reluctant gardener for whom
the 'garden in bloom' is more often 'that blooming garden.'
96 pages; Numerous engravings; Price £3.50

MY NEW FOREST HOME by Irene Soper
This account reflects a spirit of tranquillity and timelessness embodied
by the Forest itself and is a lasting testament of one who knows and
loves this memorable mandscape.
128 pages; Illustrated; Price £4.95

THE ROMANY WAY by Irene Soper
At times anecdotal, at times factual, but always sympathetic and
informative, this book is a joyous but gentle celebration of a unique people.
112 pages; Fully illustrated ; Price £4.95

LAND GIRL by Anne Hall
Her story of six years in the Women's Land Army, 1940-46
One woman's recollection of six years dedicated to the Women's Land
Army. The many photographs and the author's text combine to produce
an honest, evocative and personal portrayal of a unique chapter in our
social history.
144 pages; Illustrated throughout; Price £4.95

LUMBER JILL by Mavis Williams
Her story of four years in the Women's Timber Corps, 1942-45
A personal account of a time when women used primitive methods to
cut down trees to make pit-props for the coal mines and fuel to produce
charcoal.
96 pages; Illustrated; Price £3.95

VILLAGE PRACTICE by Anne Stratford
A Year in the life of a Country Doctor's Wife
A story told with fondness and a gentle humour – a heartwarming read.
160 pages; Illustrated; Price £4.95

POACHERS & POISONED OWLS by Romy Wyeth
Tales of a Country Policeman's Wife
This autobiographical account will appeal to a wide circle of readers.
96 pages; Illustrated; Price £4.50

WINIFRED by Sylvia Marlow
Her childhood and early working life
Winifred Spencer was born in 1899, the daughter of a cowman and his
wife and one of thirteen children. Unsentimental and honest, this is
Winifred's story of her struggle to survive.
128 pages; Illustrated throughout; Price £4.50

MAISIE & ME by Stella Ashton
A Country Childhood in the 1920s
The sights, sounds and smells of the countryside come alive in Stella
Ashton's recollections of her childhood. Words and pictures combine to
produce a loving portrait of a world past, but not forgotten.
80 pages; pen & ink drawings; Price £3.95

*These books may be obtained through your local bookshop or direct from the
publisher, post-free, at*
1 The Shambles, Bradford on Avon, Wiltshire, BA15 1JS.

*In addition to the above books, Ex Libris Press also publishes books on the West
Country and the Channel Islands. Please ask for our free illustrated list.*